What Every Principal Should Know

About Teaching Reading

How to Raise Test Scores
and Nurture a Love of Reading

MARIE CARBO

NATIONAL READING STYLES INSTITUTE
179 Lafayette Drive, Syosset, New York 11791

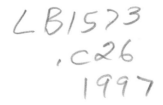

National Reading Styles Institute
179 Lafayette Drive, Syosset, New York 11791
516-921-5500 • 800-331-3117 • Fax 516-921-5591

Design by Helen Schmitz

Printed in the United States of America.

Library of Congress Cataloging-in-Publication Data

Carbo, Marie.
    What every principal should know about teaching reading: how to raise test
scores and nurture a love of reading/Marie Carbo.
      p.   cm.
    Includes bibliographical references.
    ISBN 1-883186-00-5
    1. Reading--United States. 2. School principals--United States.
    I. Title.
    LB1573.C26   1996
    372.41--dc20   96-27394
                                                               CIP

To my dear Mom, for her constant
support, friendship, and encouragement.

To my daughter Juliet, who lights
my days with her beautiful spirit.

Acknowledgements

With Special Thanks to:

Robert W. Cole, director of the Center for Accelerating Literacy (and former editor of the *Kappan* and long-time friend!), who encouraged me to write the series of articles that became this book and provided his superb editing and sage advice throughout the project.

NRSI Senior Consultant Rebecca Thomasson, who traveled and worked tirelessly over the past five years, training many of the national consultants, teachers, and administrators whose schools and classrooms appear in this book, and who added countless brilliant ideas and strategies that improved this work.

The unflappable Helen Schmitz, NRSI's delightful design artist, who took every revision with good humor and made a difficult book "user friendly" for educators.

Gail Gross and Ron Areglado of the National Association of Elementary School Principals, for their excellent advice which expanded and refined this work, making the final version more meaningful for principals.

Dorian Martin and Cade White of the Texas Elementary Principals and Supervisors Association, for publishing the original series of articles that became this book.

All the wonderful national reading styles consultants and trainers whose sizable talents and hard work translated reading styles theory into workable classroom strategies as evidenced by the photographs in this book, especially Karen Christian, Cynthia Hernandez, Barbara Hinds, Lois LaShell, and Linda Queiruga.

And, finally, to all the reading styles principals, teachers, and administrators whose dedication, hard work, courage, and intelligence provide models of best reading styles practice for the entire nation.

"A perfect reference for every principal, teacher, and parent. Up-to-date and absoluly comprehensive. A broad and insightful overview, it tells teachers exactly what to do to meet children's needs. A mammoth undertaking!"

Beverly P. Crotts, Director of Special Education, Chatham County (NC) Schools, Outstanding Administrator of the Year (1996), National Council of Administrators of Special Education

"Carbo's approach holds the greatest promise for reaching the largest number of children. Educators will find examples of outstanding programs, a wide array of specific instructional strategies, and an extensive research base to answer that most fundamental yet perpetually controversial question, 'What really works in teaching children to read?'"

Mary Renck Jalongo, Editor, Early Childhood Education Journal Professor, Indiana University of Pennsylvania

"A dynamic approach to reading instruction that explains how and why an attention to students' reading styles can bring about dramatic, rapid changes at any school. An absolute must for every principal!"

Philip Arbolino, Associate Director, Advanced Placement Program, The College Board

"An essential resource for principals! Combines many years of classroom experience with the latest research. A fantastic reference that helps teachers and principals chart a path toward success."

Nancy Cotter, Assistant Superintendent, Talladega (AL) County Schools

"A wonderful resource! User-friendly and research-based. Excellent recommendations for principals and teachers. An inspiring and encouraging 'how-to' book that can absolutely turn your school around and make life-long readers of all your students."

Heidi Mathews, Principal, Bob Hope Elementary, San Antonio, Texas

For more information about the strategies in this book and NRSI's training program, contact NRSI at 1-800-331-3117 or write at P.O. Box 737, Syosset, NY 11791.

Contents

Photo courtesy of Barbara Hinds, Bob Hope Elementary School, San Antonio, Texas.

Why Read a Book About Reading Instruction?

R eading instruction is one of the top priorities for any building principal today. Even before President Clinton made literacy a hot political issue, converging societal trends had insured that students' ability to read is a critical measure of every school's success.

"Principals face a bewildering array of trends that pose a direct threat to students' ability to learn to read."

Today's well-informed principal understands that the inability to read correlates directly with the tendency of young people to drop out of school. In fact, a study conducted by the Chicago Public Schools found lack of ability to read to be "the single most important factor in predicting which students would drop out of school" (Griffin 1987).

As if the threat of dropouts were not enough, however, principals and their teaching staff face a bewildering array of other trends that pose a direct threat to students' ability to learn to read. For example:
• An increase in the number of young people diagnosed as having a variety of learning disabilities or physical or emotional problems.
• An increase in the number of students from single-parent, no-parent, or dual-income families—in which no one may have the time, energy, or inclination to read to children or to provide other important support for learning.
• An increase in the number of high-mobility students, whose fre-

quent moves to new schools interrupt their learning and leave them without basic skills.

- An increase in the number of students with limited proficiency in English, as a result of new waves of immigration and higher birthrates among some minority groups.
- An increase in the number of students who suffer from the combined effects of poverty and/or drugs.

Inevitably, as youngsters' out-of-school problems mount, so does their difficulty in staying on track with reading and language development. All of these special conditions that face our nation's young people demand that principals and teachers possess special knowledge. They must develop an in-depth understanding of their school's reading program; they must be prepared to lead dynamic school- and district-wide efforts designed to insure that *all* students become competent, enthusiastic readers.

Too often, developing a reading program that can teach all of today's diverse and often troubled young people may seem improbable—even impossible. Consider the way reading instruction is commonly conducted: Most U.S. schools still use basal readers and workbooks as their primary reading resource. Some season that recipe for reading instruction with the addition of varying amounts of literature. Most teachers group children according to their reading levels and provide each group with different reading materials. (Some place all students in the same group with the same materials, and then try to provide differentiated instruction.) A few teachers work with students both in small groups and individually.

"The good news is that an effective solution exists—and it's being used by principals and teachers all across the United States."

Most reading systems used today provide too few choices of high-interest reading materials, too little of the reading approaches needed by individual students, and too few hands-on resources. The youngsters in our schools who are most at risk are those with reading styles mismatched by the typical reading program, as well as those who are simply bored by the materials and instruction with which they are presented.

> "Customizing reading instruction
> to students' needs and strengths
> can make the difference
> between success and failure."

The good news, though, is that an effective solution exists—and it's being used by principals and teachers all across the United States. This approach to reading instruction, known as "reading styles," allows teachers to gain a detailed understanding of their students and then identify the best way to work with each one. Rather than rely on a "one method fits all" approach—using only phonics or only whole language, for example—thousands of teachers have confirmed in their own classrooms that using different strategies to meet the needs of vastly different students is not only possible, but it is *the* most effective way to teach the full range of students in today's schools.

For some time, educators have come to accept the importance of addressing students' different learning styles. Now we are also coming to grasp the importance of working through students' different *reading styles*. A student whose teacher finds little or no success with one method of instruction can learn to read relatively easily and quickly when another, more fitting method of instruction is used. Customizing reading instruction to students' needs and strengths can make the difference between success and failure.

Throughout this book, I'll be showing you exactly how children's lives can be changed—*have* been changed—by the application of the reading styles approach. And I'll be supplementing my own explanations with detailed examples provided by principals from our network of Model Reading Styles Schools around the United States. These principals, who are now using reading styles in a wide range of schools, from rural America to the inner city, find that instructional problems caused by disruptive behavior and negative attitudes simply disappear. As Principal Diane Crawford says in the case study of her school (see Chapter 10), "I challenge you to find the emotionally disturbed children in our classrooms."

Yes, children and teachers benefit from the use of reading styles. But parents of youngsters in reading styles programs benefit, too. They see their children reading and enjoying books—often for the first time. They see them bringing home higher test scores through the efforts of teachers who are newly committed to meeting children's individual needs.

Every chapter in this little book is crammed with details of how and why an attention to students' reading styles can lead to dramatic, rapid changes at your school. Each chapter explains how your school can make the transition to using the same instructional strategies that have proven so successful nation-wide. Read along with me and find out for yourself.

What Every Principal Should Know About Teaching Reading

We want our children to become competent lifelong readers. To do this, they must learn to read well, enjoy reading, and read a lot. At the same time, we demand that students demonstrate reading competence on an ever-growing array of tests. So how do principals and teachers do both: raise test scores *and* nurture a love of reading in children?

Unfortunately, educators face enormous obstacles on the path toward these dual objectives. Ominous trends threaten to defeat our best efforts at both raising test scores and nurturing a love of reading in children (see Figure 1.1).

This first chapter will lay the foundation for bringing about high gains in reading motivation and achievement with seven basic premises and sets of recommendations for each premise.

FIGURE 1.1

Ominous trends reported in 1994 by the National Assessment of Educational Progress (NAEP) for Grades 4, 8, and 12

- U.S. students read very little, either in or outside of school.
- An overwhelming emphasis is placed on low-level reading workbook activities.
- Students have difficulty in constructing thoughtful responses when they read.
- Library use decreases throughout the grades.
- About 20% of American students report reading for fun only *yearly* or *never*.[1]

María Williams reads to her kindergartners. She uses an oversized book so that the children can see and hear the words being read.

Photo courtesy of Margil Elementary School, San Antonio I.S.D., Texas.

"The enthusiasm, interest, and delight we exhibit when we read to children are contagious."

Photo courtesy of Benson Elementary School, Uvalde, Texas.

A student volunteer models the Shared Reading Method by pointing to words as she reads them aloud to younger students. Then she and the little ones choral-read the story together.

PREMISE #1

Children Learn from Modeling

Adults and older students need to show youngsters that they value and enjoy reading. Just as young people learn language by imitation, they learn to value and enjoy reading by observing role models. The enthusiasm, interest, and delight we exhibit when we read to children are contagious. A principal with whom I work spends every spare moment of her time in classrooms, reading her favorite books to students. In her school, the students have begun to check more and more books out of the library and read them avidly.

That principal's message to her students is strong and positive: Reading is fun! I loved it when I was your age, and I want you to enjoy it as much as I did. Clearly, here is a role model that can provoke a heightened interest in lifelong reading.

One important point: The recommendations that accompany every premise in this chapter are intended for both principals and teachers (and parents, too!). Helping children succeed as readers is a team effort.

Recommendations for Modeling

- As time permits, read to groups or classes of students.
- Encourage the teachers to read aloud to their class *at least* 15 minutes daily.
- Stress the use of modeling techniques for emerging readers. Have teachers read large charts and books while pointing to words and then phrases. Encourage the use of many short stories dictated by the children. Provide training for the teacher, if needed.
- For non-fluent readers, encourage teachers to read aloud a short passage a few times while the children follow along in their books, until students can read the passage independently.
- Assist financially in providing books on tape that allow students to listen and follow along. Both textbooks and stories should be recorded. Students need to hear and see words repeatedly.[2] Place the recordings in classroom listening centers. Rotate the books and tapes among classrooms (see Chapter 5).

Lots of high-interest books are available for students to choose.

Photo courtesy of Roosevelt Elementary School in Medford, Oregon.

Second-graders listen intently to a story.

Photo courtesy of Mike Kasnic, Butcher Children's School, Emporia, Kansas.

This fourth-grade book club is based on similar reading interests.

Photo courtesy of Mike Kasnic, Butcher Children's School, Emporia, Kansas.

PREMISE #2

It's Natural for Children to Enjoy Reading and to be Motivated to Read

The principal I just mentioned wisely tapped into children's natural curiosity and motivation for reading. The simple act of reading aloud something we enjoy has always been one of the most powerful ways to interest children in reading.

"Engaging a child's natural motivation to read increases reading enjoyment and places him or her on the path to becoming a lifelong reader."

It's the job of schools to make reading enjoyable and motivating—to bring out the children's natural interests and curiosity and to encourage new interests. Engaging a child's natural motivation to read increases reading enjoyment and places him or her on the path to becoming a lifelong reader. Highly motivated students become more responsible about reading and are more likely to practice reading regularly.

Recommendations for Motivating Students

- Schedule a variety of people to read to students often (teachers, authors, the principal, parents, and older students).
- Provide a wide choice of reading materials in every classroom based on students' interests.
- Support the formation of book clubs that meet regularly. Allow students to create bulletin boards that reflect their reading interests.
- Provide opportunities for students to discuss their favorite books, characters, and events.

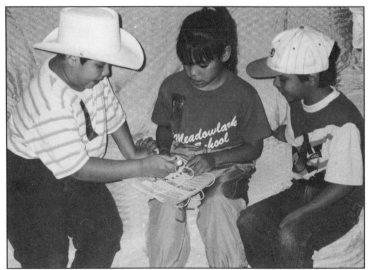

Photo courtesy of Robb Elementary School, Uvalde, Texas.

In Mrs. Muñoz's second grade, listening to recordings of stories and doing reading work with friends makes learning to read easy and fun.

Photo courtesy of Spokane Public Schools, Washington.

Two students listen to the same story before joining their reading group.

PREMISE #3

Learning to Read Should be Easy and Fun

Modeling for students (Premise #1) and motivating them to read (Premise #2) are the first steps toward literacy. What about those youngsters who don't become fluent readers quickly? For them, there is a danger that reading may become a struggle. When the process of learning to read becomes laborious and even embarrassing, then the chances are high that the child will dislike and avoid reading.

Our aim should be to help all children feel comfortable and relaxed when they are learning to read, to avoid creating *any* sense of failure, and to provide the amount and kind of practice needed to move kids forward. Here are six initial strategies that can help.

Recommendations for Making Reading Easy and Fun

- Help teachers and parent-support groups to provide cozy reading areas with lots of high-interest books, soft furniture, rugs, and pillows. Help students to associate reading with pleasure.
- Provide time for students to read with friends — including cross-age or cross-classroom friends.
- Encourage the development of a library of specially recorded books. Record high-interest stories using a slightly slower-than-usual pace. Place a short passage on a tape side (about two minutes). Have emerging readers listen to the tape and follow along a few times before reading the passage aloud (see Chapters 4 and 5).
- Suggest that teachers allow their students to practice passages *before* reading in a group.
- Encourage teachers to accommodate their students' reading styles by allowing children choices of how they will demonstrate what they have read, such as through pantomime, discussion, drawing, or writing.
- Become familiar with a variety of reading methods so you can help teachers use methods that accommodate their students' strengths.

Provide cozy reading areas with lots of high-interest books, soft furniture, rugs, and pillows. Help students to associate reading with pleasure.

Photo courtesy of Barbara Hinds, Bob Hope Elementary School, San Antonio, Texas.

Photo courtesy of Knight Elementary School, Lilburn, Georgia.

Photo courtesy of Lois LaShell, Lake Stevens S.D., Washington.

Photo courtesy of Mike Kasnic, Butcher Children's School, Emporia, Kansas.

PREMISE #4

Good Readers Spend Time Practicing Reading

Let's assume that we have motivated children to read. They have heard many excellent and inspiring reading models, and we have made the process of learning to read easy and fun. What's the next step?

Practice, practice, practice. Good readers spend a lot of time reading. Yet most American children spend very little time reading anything at all. Practice helps to improve reading comprehension and vocabulary; practice also helps to raise test scores. To encourage students to read, we need to provide both high-interest reading materials and the time to read them.

Recommendations for Facilitating Reading Practice

• Encourage children to take books to read at home.
• Set aside specific, uninterrupted reading periods during the school day.
• Have available inventories that assess students' reading interests. Provide teachers with reading material based on those interests.
• Provide a wide variety of books for different reading interests and reading levels.
• Have taped books available for those who are not yet independent readers.
• Sell affordable books.
• Sponsor book exchanges that allow children to trade books.
• Suggest to your faculty that they de-emphasize workbook activities. If necessary, provide training for teachers in alternative learning activities to replace the workbook (see Chapter 6). Children need to spend most of their reading time reading, being read to, discussing what they have read, and writing about what they have read.

PREMISE #5

Literacy-Rich Environments
Increase Reading Motivation

Providing choices of high-interest reading materials is a strong motivator. Students tend to read for longer periods when they enjoy what they're reading. Emerging readers benefit from at least some reading materials that reflect their cultural, linguistic, and socioeconomic backgrounds.

Initially, easy materials can be used that ensure success, such as big books, picture books, recorded books, children's own stories, and books with predictable language and repetitive phrases. Children need a wide variety of reading resources, especially high-quality children's literature.

Recommendations for Creating Literacy-Rich Environments

- Identify students' interests through questionnaires and interviews. Provide reading materials based on those interests.
- Label objects and post written charts throughout the school, including classrooms, cafeteria, halls, your office, media center, etc.
- Stock well-organized libraries with a wide variety of quality reading materials ranging from easy to challenging levels.
- Include an array of types of reading materials, such as poetry, storybooks, books written by children, children's newspapers and magazines, recorded books, reading games, and software.

Photo courtesy of Roanoke Public Schools, Virginia.

A well-organized and well-stocked library is a strong motivation for reading. Note the variety of reading areas. The excellent display of book covers entices children to open the books and explore them.

PREMISE #6

Active Participation by Parents Promotes Literacy

Parents and guardians are a valuable resource for schools. They can create materials, listen to children read, run book fairs, and use modeling methods (Chapter 4) to help children become fluent readers.

Workshops can be offered at convenient times to help parents understand the importance of reading in the home, demonstrate techniques for reading aloud, using recorded books and hands-on materials, and so on.

Recommendations for Increasing Active Participation

- Hold workshops regularly at convenient times. Provide snacks and time for socializing and bonding.
- Provide information about reading styles, especially the importance of accommodating students' perceptual strengths (visual, auditory, tactile, kinesthetic — see Chapter 3).
- Provide helpful reading information for parents depending on their needs. Examples: lists of recommended children's books, procedures for securing library cards, creating good reading environments in the home, and suggestions for reading aloud to children.
- Teach parents and guardians a variety of modeling strategies for increasing reading fluency and comprehension.
- Discuss and read excerpts from exemplary children's literature, and distribute lists of books.
- Demonstrate simple questioning strategies that stimulate language and thinking.
- Have a "read in." These are often held in the evening. Parents, guardians, teachers, and the principal read to small groups of children. Create a relaxed atmosphere with some blankets, stuffed animals, and snacks.

PREMISE #7

Stretching Students with High-Level Reading Materials Increases Reading Ability

All the recommendations thus far are designed to put children on the path to becoming good readers. If we do not expose our youngsters to high-level materials, however, it's likely that they'll never be able to read or understand them. This stretching process needs to be done so that children are challenged, but not defeated.

Stretching occurs too rarely in compensatory or remedial programs, even though students would "benefit greatly from increased expectations and demands," according to a report by Anderson and Pellicer. These two researchers evaluated U.S. programs designed to improve the achievement of economically disadvantaged and educationally deficient students.[3] We spend billions of dollars each year on Title I programs, and yet many youngsters in these programs do not do well in reading.

"We need to stretch children so that they are challenged, but not defeated."

Recommendations for Stretching Readers

- Suggest that teachers read aloud challenging materials often, and ask thought-provoking questions.
- Solicit parental and community help in providing real situations that challenge children's thinking, such as running a toy sale or planning a trip.
- Encourage teachers to foster thinking skills by asking high-level questions, such as predicting or interpreting the behavior of characters in a story.
- Have teachers practice how they will model high-level thinking by actually thinking aloud about questions relating to something that has been read.
- Encourage teachers to have their students design their own high-level questions.

After all of these premises and recommendations, what do good reading programs actually look like? As described by the National Assessment of Educational Progress (NAEP), reading programs that provide optimum learning conditions for emerging readers have five charac-

Photo courtesy of Robb Elementary School, Uvalde, Texas.

Outdoor reading with Title I teacher, Mr. Guzman makes learning to read fun.

teristics (see Figure 1.2). These characteristics are given strong support by implementing the seven major premises in this chapter.

The next chapter will tackle the controversy of whole language versus phonics. It will emphasize the dangers of becoming caught in the pendulum swings of the debate between these two camps in the field of reading. Chapter 2 focuses on the child instead of on any single method, discussing the utility and the weaknesses of both approaches—how to plug the holes, combine them, and make them stronger instructionally.

FIGURE 1.2

Optimum Learning Conditions for Emerging Readers (National Assessment of Educational Progress)

1. Students do large amounts of reading both in and outside of school; they read a great variety of materials (novels, poems, and stories).
2. Workbook activities are deemphasized.
3. Discussions of reading materials emphasize high-level thinking.
4. Reading and writing are connected.
5. Literacy is supported in the home.

LINKING IMPORTANT RESEARCH

Reading Rated Most Important Subject

A national survey reported in 1995 found that the basic skills of reading and writing were rated as the most "absolutely essential" subjects that local public schools should concentrate on. These basic skills were rated as more essential than "computer skills," "honesty," "tolerance," "drugs," and "good citizenship."[4]

What Determines Success in Jobs and Careers?

"Persistence" and "inner drive" were rated the most important factors for determining success by the public, parents, teachers, and leaders. Experiences that lead to persistence and inner drive are those that enable a child to be successful. Success in reading correlates strongly to reading motivation and competence. If students are not motivated to read, they read very little. If they read very little, it is unlikely that they will become successful, competent readers; without those experiences, it is unlikely that they will have strong inner drive and persistence.[5]

What Motivates Students to Read?

Since the amount of reading that children do is directly related to their level of motivation, what does motivate children to read? The answers are not surprising and can be found in a synthesis of the research on motivation. Here are three important factors:

- Prior experiences with a book ("My mom or teacher read it to me" or "I saw it on TV").
- Social interactions about books (hearing about a book from friends, parents or teachers.
- Book choice (self-selection of books).[6]

REFERENCES

1. *1994 NAEP Reading: A First Look, Findings from the National Assessment of Educational Progress* (Washington, D.C.: U.S. Education Department, Office of Educational Research and Improvement, 1994).

2. M. Carbo, *How to Record Books for Maximum Reading Gains* (Syosset, N.Y.: NRSI, 1989).

3. L. W. Anderson and L. O. Pellicer, "Synthesis of Research on Compensatory and Remedial Education," *Educational Leadership,* September 1990, pp. 10-16.

4. J. Johnson, *Assignment Incomplete: The Unfinished Business of Education Reform* (New York: Public Agenda, 1995).

5. Ibid.

6. P. Koskinen et al., "In Their Own Words: What Elementary Students Have to Say About Motivation to Read," *The Reading Teacher,* vol. 48, 1994, pp. 176-78.

Ah! A beanbag near a pillowed tub. Yes, this is a classroom!

Photo courtesy of Lois Lashell, Lake Stevens S.D., Washington.

Photo courtesy of Howard County Schools, Maryland.

Playing reading games with a friend makes learning skills fun.

Photo courtesy of Mike Kasnic, Butcher Children's School, Emporia, Kansas.

When provided seating choices, some children choose to sit at a desk while others prefer a more informal reading environment.

Special places and special books help to develop life-long readers.

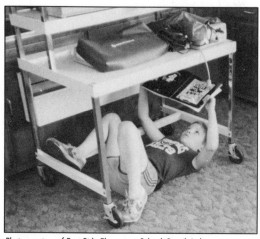

Photo courtesy of East Side Elementary School, Brazil, Indiana.

Sometimes it takes imagination to find an unclaimed, private place to read.

Photo courtesy of Roosevelt Elementary School, Medford, Oregon.

This second-grader reads with her book and her water bottle. She likes to rock and read.

CHAPTER 2

Whole Language
vs. Phonics

Make no mistake: Reading is big business, and the stakes are astronomical. Children who don't read well are in grave danger of doing poorly in school and eventually dropping out. Because success in reading is so terribly important, schools face unrelenting pressure to produce high test scores.

This chapter will tackle the continuing controversy of whole language versus phonics. I'll emphasize the need to avoid being caught up in the pendulum swings between these two camps. Instead, in focusing on the child, I'll discuss both systems—how to plug the holes in them, combine the two approaches, and make them stronger instructional tools.

> "Because success in reading is so terribly important, schools face unrelenting pressure to produce high test scores."

High Stakes, Big Claims—and Too Little Research

Principals and teachers are expected to accomplish wonders in reading. Unfortunately, the high stakes involved seem to bring out the worst in many would-be providers of support. Products like "Hooked on Phonics" make it appear easy to teach anyone to read. Recently, however, after a whopping $200 million in sales, "Hooked on Phonics" was cited by the Federal Trade Commission for false advertising and insufficient research.[1]

Nor do the claims of superiority by advocates of phonics appear to be based on sound research. I evaluated the original phonics studies reported in the literature over a 70-year period. My findings disclosed that most of these studies had been poorly conceived and executed and/or their positive results had been erroneously reported.[2] My findings were extensively reported in *Phi Delta Kappan* and corroborated by Richard Turner, a noted researcher and former vice president of the American Educational Research Association. Turner reported in *Phi Delta Kappan* that:

> [S]ystematic phonics falls into that vast category of weak instructional treatments with which education is perennially plagued.... Perhaps it is time for reading experts to turn away from the debate over systematic phonics in search of more powerful instructional treatments for beginning reading....[3]

"The truth is that some children do learn to read easily with phonics—and some do not. The same can be said of whole language programs."

More recently, articles in *Education Week* have criticized both Reading Recovery and whole language for insufficient data.[4]

The truth is that some children do learn to read easily with phonics—and some do not. The same can be said of whole-language programs. *Principals need to understand both systems and use the best of both, along with other effective reading programs.* As the instructional leader in their building, principals can provide the training and assistance teachers need so that a variety of reading methods are used to help students read easily and well.

Danger: Pendulum Swing Approaching!

People have been searching for *the* single best way to teach all children to read for more than a century. No matter which approach to teaching reading enjoys popularity, reading failures persist, disillusionment spreads, and the pendulum swings to yet another approach.

High stakes only make the pendulum swing ever faster. The

"look-say" method held sway for about 30 years (1940-1970) before the pendulum swung to phonics. Phonics was popular for the next 20 years (1970-1990), and then whole language gained a strong foothold. Within a few years whole language came under fire, especially by advocates of phonics.

Amazingly, some approaches to reading are tried for as little as a year or two and then discarded if scores fail to rise dramatically. Too little funding available to train teachers in new methods, combined with a desperate need for quick successes, make a bad combination.

Analytic vs. Global Pendulum Swings

The occurrence of these pendulum swings is predictable, and so is their direction. When a global approach to reading enjoys popularity for a time ("look-say," for example), the pendulum then swings back to a more analytic approach, such as phonics. The resulting heated debates should come as no surprise.

> "We must understand both the analytic and the global models of teaching reading if we hope to improve reading instruction."

People who believe fervently in global approaches to reading usually disbelieve analytic approaches passionately—and vice versa. Our emotions prevent us from making rational, reasoned decisions about *what is best for young people*. The debaters pit one reading approach against another—sometimes making exaggerated or false claims and counter-claims. In the process, the focus of the "great debate" moves away from where it must be: on the individual child. We must understand *both* the analytic and the global models of teaching reading if we hope to improve reading instruction.

Focus on Literature, Choice, Fun, and Small Amounts of Phonics

It's generally not advisable to use a single approach to reading exclusively. Many combinations are necessary to accommodate the different learning styles for reading, or "reading styles," that are usually found within a single classroom.

Having conducted extensive research on children's reading styles, I advocate *selecting an approach that matches the style of the student.* Since young children and poor readers generally exhibit more global than analytic characteristics, an extensive body of reading styles research supports whole language as a *framework* for reading instruction—but only as a framework. The strategies within that framework depend on the reading styles of the particular students in the group. Reading instruction should focus on literature, choices, fun, and writing, with some direct instruction in phonics for those youngsters who learn well with that approach.

The Analytic Model

The analytic model of teaching reading moves from the parts to the whole, in the same way that phonics is taught (see Figure 2.1). The first stage requires mastery of isolated letter sounds. In Stage 2, students practice letter sounds by reading words containing the learned sounds. Next they read connected text, or stories. This approach regards a knowledge of letter sounds as a critical skill for all learners.

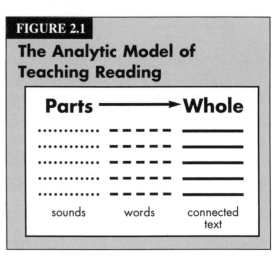

FIGURE 2.1

The Analytic Model of Teaching Reading

Parts ———→ Whole

sounds   words   connected text

Phonics: Who Succeeds? Who Fails?

Youngsters who do well with phonics tend to have strongly auditory and analytic reading styles. Children who are auditory can hear and remember letter sounds. If they are also analytic, the logic of phonics makes sense to them, for they proceed naturally from bits of information to the whole. Phonics instruction is usually highly sequential, organized, direct, and predictable—all conditions that appeal to analytics.

But phonics can be confusing and boring to students who are not analytic, who don't learn easily when information is presented in small portions, step by step. As indicated in reading styles research, the majority of young children are global, not analytic, learners. Moreover, there is great danger in over-emphasizing phonics. Even the most analytic youngsters need a reading program that emphasizes *literature*. The most serious problems arise for students who are not sufficiently auditory to learn or to blend letter sounds. These students find phonics difficult or impossible to learn. If children cannot *hear* the differences among sounds, then they cannot associate those sounds with their corresponding letters. This situation is similar to that of a tone-deaf person who can't repeat a tone. Being sound-deaf can create years of problems—that is, if a youngster is exposed primarily to phonics instruction.

The Global Model

The global model of teaching reading moves from the whole to the parts, in the same way that whole language is taught (see Figure 2.2). In Stage 1, large amounts of connected text are read aloud to students repeatedly. After the children can read the stories independently, they move to Stage 2, in which they practice words and phrases from the stories in isolation. In Stage 3, the teacher uses some phonics, often by encouraging children to "discover" similarities in words they have encountered in their reading and writing.

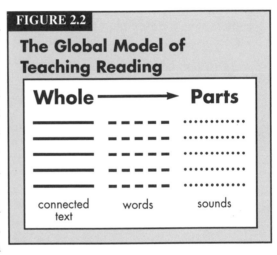

FIGURE 2.2

The Global Model of Teaching Reading

Whole ⟶ Parts

connected text · words · sounds

An understanding of individual reading styles will clarify what type of learner is likely to succeed or fail using each reading approach. Students have different strengths and weaknesses; every reading approach demands certain reading style strengths of the learner.

Whole Language: Who Succeeds? Who Fails?

Children who do well in whole-language programs tend to have visual, tactile, and global reading styles. They can recall words they see and hear repeatedly in high-interest stories. Lots of experience with story writing helps tactile learners to remember words they have felt as they write them. Whole-language programs usually emphasize fun, literature, hands-on learning, and peer interactions—all conditions that appeal to global learners.

But whole language can feel disorganized and haphazard to analytic learners. If the modeling of stories is too infrequent or if the teacher does not provide enough interesting repetition, such youngsters can fall behind quickly. Since the *systematic* teaching of phonics is not emphasized, some children may not develop the tools they need for decoding words. Finally, such strategies as invented spelling may confuse analytic youngsters who want to use correct spellings, or children with memory deficits who are likely to persist in their invented spellings long past the early grades. Even children with good memories may have difficulty transitioning to traditional spellings if invented spelling is used for too long a period of time.

> "Remember, phonics is only one of many reading methods. Try recorded books, for example, or story writing."

Photo courtesy of Robb Elementary School, Uvalde, Texas.

This chart describes which reading style matches each reading method. Hung in a classroom, it provides a quick check for the teacher.

Recommendations for Principals

Here are eight ways to improve most reading programs in the shortest possible time. These suggestions combine the best of phonics, whole language, and reading styles.

1. Emphasize the fun of

Photo courtesy of Lycoming Valley Middle School, Pennsylvania.

A high-interest reading game based on their book is enjoyed by Marilyn Gardner's students.

reading. Fill hallway bulletin boards with exciting reading displays: paintings of book characters, children's written imitations of such writers as Dr. Seuss, sign-up sheets for book clubs.

Photo courtesy of Roosevelt Elementary School, Medford, Oregon.

Here's a super strategy for kinesthetic learners. Just write a story on pieces of construction paper, add drawings, then laminate. Here the children play "Scoot Story." With each scoot forward, they read a part of the story.

2. *Do not* allow youngsters to be referred to special education classes simply because they can't learn with a particular reading method. Make sure that other reading approaches are given an honest try first.

3. Help teachers to accumulate the books and shelving needed for classroom libraries, and any other needed materials.

4. Encourage reading aloud to children daily. Try to get into classrooms and read to children yourself as often as possible. Ask children what their favorite books are and how many books they've read. Demonstrate your enthusiasm for reading.

5. Purchase tape players and blank cassettes so that books can be recorded for youngsters. Children can listen to the tapes while looking at the words. This extra modeling is especially important for young people with limited proficiency in English, those who have been read to very little, or children who simply need

repetition to help them learn (see Chapter 5).

6. Recruit older children to make reading games for younger ones, including phonics games.

7. Send teachers who are "movers and shakers" to some good reading seminars during the year. Follow up with meetings so that the best ideas are shared and *used.*

Recommendations for Teachers

Here are some specific recommendations for improving phonics and whole-language programs and ways to combine the best of both.

To Improve Phonics Programs

• Make the focus literature and fun. Read to your students often, choral-read with them, and give them time to read both alone and in pairs.

• Guard against one of the most negative side effects of phonics: boredom. Be careful not to overdo phonics or worksheets. Spend only five to 30 minutes in one day on phonics if needed; do few, if any, worksheets daily; allow children to work together.

• Include many games in your teaching. For most children, phonics is easier to learn if they are having fun and are not placed under stress.

• If your students are not able to learn phonics with a fair degree of ease, try other approaches. Remember, *phonics is only one of many reading methods.* Try recorded books, for example, or story writing.

• Develop a well-stocked library in your classroom. Give children time to browse, read, and discuss books.

To Improve Whole-Language Programs

• Continue to emphasize literature and fun while providing adequate structure and some step-by-step skill work, especially for analytic students.

• Provide sufficient tools for decoding words. Use small amounts of direct instruction in phonics for auditory and analytic learners. Try tape-recording phonics lessons so that students can work independently to improve these skills.

• Include games in your teaching. Since most young children are tactile, they often learn words and skills quickly with hands-on games.

- Don't use invented spelling for extensive periods, especially with strongly analytic learners or with students who have memory problems.
- Provide sufficient modeling of reading aloud for children not yet able to read independently or in pairs. Use large amounts of shared reading, choral reading, and recorded books as necessary (see Chapter 4).

Chapter 3 will show you how to identify and capitalize on reading style strengths. I'll begin by explaining what reading styles are; then I'll discuss some simple steps toward observing and accommodating children's differing reading styles, identifying styles with the Reading Style Inventory®, and observing reading styles in action.

"Children can listen to the tapes while looking at the words. This extra modeling is especially important for young people with limited proficiency in English, those who have been read to very little, or children who simply need repetition to help them learn."

Photo courtesy of Roosevelt Elementary School, Medford, Oregon.

The modeling provided by these special recordings helps to increase word recognition and fluency (see Chapter 5).

REFERENCES

1. "Phonics Ads Cited," *Newsday,* December 15, 1994, p. A64; "Hooked on Hype," *Dateline*, NBC-TV, December 13, 1994.

2. M. Carbo, "Debunking the Great Phonics Myth," *Phi Delta Kappan,* vol. 70, 1988, pp. 226-40.

3. Richard L. Turner, "The 'Great' Debate—Can Both Carbo and Chall Be Right?" *Phi Delta Kappan*, December 1989, pp. 276-83.

4. Debra Viadero, "Report Casts Critical Eye on Reading Recovery Program," *Education Week*, December 7, 1994; and Robert Rothman, "Studies Cast Doubt on Benefits of Using Only Whole Language to Teach Reading," *Education Week*, January 8, 1992.

Photo courtesy of Robb Elementary School, Uvalde, Texas.

Learning to read should be easy and fun. Use lots of hands-on materials that relate to holistic themes for tactile/kinesthetic students.

A relaxing, comfortable, nurturing reading environment reduces stress and increases the mind's ability to learn.

Photo courtesy of Sacred Heart Academy, Hempstead, New York.

This youngster reads best in a quiet, informal reading environment.

Photo courtesy of Stemley Road Elementary School, Talladega, Alabama.

Most young children prefer to read in an informal area. This tent makes it feel like a reading camp-out.

"Not only does every person have a distinctly different reading style, but every reading method, resource, and strategy demands particular reading style strengths of the learner."

Photo courtesy of Roanoke County Schools, Virginia.

This kinesthetic child concentrates better when he can touch and move the sentence parts.

Photo courtesy of Stemley Road Elementary School, Talladega, Alabama.

Lots of tactile stimulation helps these tactile children recall their words (writing words with a wooden dowel in clay, then tracing over the indentations with their fingers).

Strengthening Reading Programs with Reading Styles

P lace two children of similar backgrounds and intelligence in the same reading class. Both are attentive, well-behaved, and enthusiastic about learning to read. Have the teacher follow exactly the teacher's guide for the reading program. One child learns to read while the other does not. Why? It is probable that the teacher matched the reading style of the successful reader while mismatching the style of the child who did not learn to read.

"When teachers match, rather than mismatch, their students' reading styles, learning to read becomes easier, motivation increases, and achievement improves."

By placing the focus where it needs to be—on the individual child—principals and teachers can avoid becoming caught up in the needless pendulum swings and time-wasting debates about *the* best approach to teaching reading. There does not appear to be one best method; there seems to be only the method that best suits the strengths and reading style of each learner.

Knowing how to capitalize on students' reading styles is a big step to providing effective instruction in reading—instruction that minimizes the chance of failure. When teachers match, rather than mismatch, their students' reading styles, learning to read becomes easier, motivation increases, and achievement improves. Even at-risk students have made gains ten times greater than their previous progress.[1]

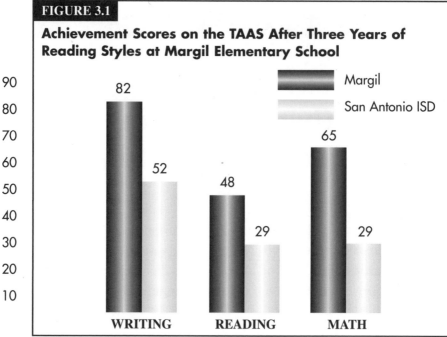

FIGURE 3.1

Achievement Scores on the TAAS After Three Years of Reading Styles at Margil Elementary School

After two years of reading styles training, Margil Elementary School moved from 61st out of 65 schools academically to ninth in the district. After three years of reading styles training, Margil surpassed district scores in all basic subjects on the Texas Assessment of Academic Skills (TAAS).
Source: San Antonio (TX) I.S.D., 1993.

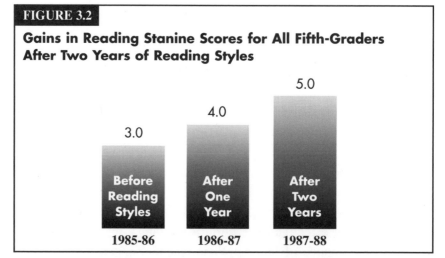

FIGURE 3.2

Gains in Reading Stanine Scores for All Fifth-Graders After Two Years of Reading Styles

In the summer of 1986, a small group of educators from Bledsoe County (TN) attended the National Reading Styles Conference. More teachers were trained at the 1987 annual conference. Students of the participating teachers advanced two stanines in reading over the two-year period. Bledsoe County won the Governor's Award for Educational Excellence. (See Snyder, 1994.)

What's a Reading Style?

A person's reading style is his or her special learning style for reading. Reading style focuses on a person's needs and strengths *during the act of reading.* We can identify a person's reading style with a high degree of accuracy.

Reading styles consider how a student's ability to learn to read is affected by the (1) reading environment, and the reader's (2) emotional make-up, (3) sociological preferences, (4) physical needs, and (5) style of processing information. Not only does every person have a distinctly different reading style, but every reading method, resource, and strategy demands particular reading style strengths of the learner.

Results of Reading Styles Programs

During the past decade, teaching grounded in the reading styles model has demonstrated the power to bring about rapid results with youngsters. Consider these examples:

- Within two years, Margil Elementary School, an inner-city school in San Antonio, Texas, rose from 61st place to ninth academically among the district's 65 elementary schools. The following year, Margil surpassed district averages in all basic subjects. As a result, reading styles spread to 37 San Antonio elementary schools—on a voluntary basis.
- In 1985, the schools in Bledsoe County, Tennessee, averaged a stanine score of only 3 in reading—not unusual for a rural school in a poverty area. Three years later, Bledsoe schools rose by two stanines in reading, equaling state and national averages. For its progress, the district received the Governor's Award for Educational Excellence.

What improved these students' achievement so dramatically? At all of the schools involved, teachers based their styles of reading instruction on each student's strengths and needs. In other words, *students' needs drive instruction*—not an outside system of teaching or a set of commercial materials.

FIGURE 3.3

Accommodating Reading Styles

Visual	Students with Perceptual Strengths Can Easily:	Enjoy/Learn Best by:	Learn to Read Best:
	• Recall what they see • Follow written or drawn instructions • Learn by observing people, objects, pictures, etc.	Using computer graphics; performing visual puzzles; looking at or designing maps, charts, graphs, diagrams, cartoons, posters, bulletin boards	With sight methods, dissimilar words, silent reading, words accompanied by pictures or slides, stories in filmstrips or videos
Auditory	• Recall what they hear • Follow spoken instructions • Learn by listening and speaking	Talking, interviewing, debating, participating on a panel, asking and answering questions, memorizing, making oral reports	With phonics, choral reading, by listening to stories and recordings of books, discussing stories, reading orally
Tactile	• Recall what they touch • Follow instructions they write or touch • Learn by touching or manipulating objects	Doodling, sketching, playing board games, building models, constructing dioramas and relief maps, setting up experiments, writing, tracing	With writing/tracing methods, such as Fernald, language experience. By playing games or reading instructions, then making something
Kinesthetic	• Recall what they experience • Follow instructions that they perform or rehearse • Learn when engaged in physical activity	Playing floor games, assembling and/or disassembling objects, building models, participating in fairs, setting up experiments, acting, role playing, scavenger hunts	By pantomiming, acting in plays, riding a stationary bike while listening to a book, recording and reading, reading instructions and then building/doing something
Global	Tendencies Often: • Make decisions based on emotions and intuition • Are spontaneous, random • Focus on creativity • Care less about a tidy environment	Enjoy/Learn Best with: Information presented in an interesting or humorous story, examples, interesting materials, group work, and activities	Learn to Read Best: With holistic reading methods, such as recorded books, story writing, choral reading, with books, computer software, audiovisual materials, projects, and games
Analytic	Often: • Make decisions based on logic or common sense • Plan and organize well • Focus on details and facts • Like a tidy environment	Information presented in sequential steps, with rules and examples, structured materials, teacher-directed lessons, clear goals and requirements	Phonics (if auditory) programmed materials, puzzles, some worksheets—reinforced by strategies appropriate for global learners

©Marie Carbo, 1995

The Importance of Identifying Reading Styles

Suppose a second-grade teacher balances her reading program with equal amounts of phonics and whole-language strategies. Is she pursuing the best possible strategy for her students? Probably not, according to research in reading styles. The reading style of most second-graders is a better match with global approaches, so she should probably be using more holistic strategies rather than analytic and auditory ones (such as phonics).

But what of this *particular* bunch of second-graders? What we know of the reading styles of most second-graders helps, but maybe this class is unusual. Perhaps it contains many analytic/auditory learners. Maybe the teacher should place more emphasis on phonics. To know for sure, we would need to identify the reading style of each child, or at least those most at risk of failure.

How to Identify Individual Reading Styles

Let's begin with a simple way to identify students' reading styles: by watching the students! Teachers can identify patterns of behavior. When students choose to do something in the same way repeatedly, such choices provide a strong indication of the student's preferred style. For example, youngsters who shift in their seats constantly probably need greater mobility; they may be kinesthetic learners, who learn well through body movement. Children who recall what they hear very well, who like read-aloud stories and directions, may be highly auditory; that is, they may learn best by listening.

A good technique for observing children's behavior is to provide them with acceptable choices. This is also the easiest way to accommodate differences within a classroom. Here are three examples:

- *To identify sociological preferences*: "You may do this activity alone, with a partner, or in a small group."
- *To identify preferred reading environment*: "Choose one of the three reading areas—wherever you feel most comfortable and can do your best."
- *To identify perceptual strengths:* "Describe your favorite scene in this story. You may draw or write about it (visual/tactile), pantomime it (kinesthetic), or discuss it (auditory)."

FIGURE 3.4

Individual Reading Style Profile

Melinda's RSI Individual Profile describes her reading style and compatible reading approaches. The RSI disk also produces a more detailed three-page report and prints descriptions of each of the reading methods recommended.[2]

STUDENT NAME: MELINDA A.   TEACHER:
DATE OF PROFILE: 1/25/95   GRADE: 4   BIRTHDATE: 10/4/85

GLOBAL/ANALYTIC TENDENCIES
Strong global tendencies
Minimal analytic tendencies

PERCEPTUAL STRENGTHS
Minimal auditory strengths
Minimal visual strengths
Good tactile strengths
Excellent kinesthic strengths

RECOMMENDED READING METHODS
Fernald method
Carbo Recorded-Book method
Modeling methods

RECOMMENDED READING MATERIALS
Manipulatives with large-muscle movement, floor games
Writing materials, eg., writing books, typewriters
"Hands-on" activities

RECOMMENDED TEACHING STRATEGIES
Allow student demonstrations
Include writing, drawing, games
Use high-interest stories
Provide colored overlays; use large print
Limit true/false, multiple-choice items

Using the Reading Style Inventory® (RSI)

For more detailed information about a youngster's reading style, a diagnostic questionnaire called the Reading Style Inventory®, or RSI, is available. The RSI program produces computerized reports that describe a student's reading style and list the methods, materials, and strategies that capitalize on that style.

Melinda's report in Figure 3.4 tells us that she is strongly global and minimally analytic, highly tactile and kinesthetic, and needs to use the Fernald Method, the Carbo Recorded-Book® Method, modeling, and hands-on materials for the greatest reading gains.

Accommodating Students' Reading Styles

What does a classroom look like when students' reading styles are accommodated? Many elementary children are:

• *Global—they need to be emotionally involved in learning;*
• *Tactile—they're hands-on learners; and*
• *Kinesthetic—they learn through whole-body movement. They also tend to have high needs for mobility and a strong preference for reading on soft furniture in a quiet, organized environment.*

Teachers can accommodate these reading styles by including in their classroom: some soft cushioned seating and dimly lit reading areas, learning centers, and a variety of reading materials, including books on tape, a well-stocked classroom library, and hands-on materials. The teacher should consider using a variety of approaches to teaching reading, and the children can work in many different groupings, as well as reading alone.

Given a choice of how to describe their favorite scene in a story, these second-graders in Mrs. Backor's class decided to draw it (visual/tactile) and then discuss it (auditory).

Photo courtesy of Robb Elementary School, Uvalde, Texas.

Recommendations for Principals

- Use the Reading Style Inventory® (RSI) to identify the reading styles of students, especially those most at risk.
- Encourage an awareness of different styles in a variety of ways. You might have classes draw and share pictures about where they like to read and with whom. Place a bulletin board about students' reading styles in the front hallway.
- I made this point earlier, but it bears repeating: Don't allow youngsters to be referred to special education or remedial classes simply because they can't learn with a particular reading method. Make sure that other reading methods have been given an honest try first. Use the Reading Style Inventory® as a part of the information gathered for suggested classroom modification by the school's intervention team.
- Try to schedule reading at the time of day that most students are alert. Note that many "underachievers" have more energy during late morning, not early morning.
- Arrange for older children or volunteers to make reading games (including phonics games) for younger students. Suggest that the teachers use games more frequently than worksheets (see Chapter 6).
- Purchase tape recorders and blank tape cassettes so that books can be recorded for youngsters. Encourage teachers to use the recorded books often with students who are at risk of reading failure (see Chapter 5).

- Try to stock a large variety of reading games, recorded books, and high-interest books. Locate and coordinate the reading materials you have. Decide what types you need. Have them created or order them if you can.

Not only is this kinesthetic student releasing pent-up energy, but learning and motivation are accelerating as well.

- Attend training sessions on reading styles with a team from your building.
- Discuss students' styles with teachers—and ways of capitalizing on those styles (see Figure 3.3).

- Make the accommodation of students' reading styles a building-wide objective. Have each teacher select one reading style strategy to implement using the following list of recommendations for teachers.

Recommendations for Teachers

- When one method or strategy isn't working, try another approach. Try to match each youngster's strengths and interests as consistently as possible.
- During reading, try turning off half the lights if possible, and then permit children to choose where they will read. Those who are light-sensitive can experience discomfort in bright light.
- Allow students with visual problems to try placing colored overlays over a page of print. If that technique makes the words seem clearer or more stable on the page, permit the student to continue using the overlay.
- Let students decide—at least sometimes—with whom they wish to read, making certain that they understand that their choice has to make it easier for them to read and learn and that their behavior cannot impinge on their classmates' reading style. In other words, if two youngsters need to process information by discussing, this should be done quietly and away from those who need quiet to learn best.
- Give students many choices of ways to do a book report. This helps to accommodate different modalities, e.g., pantomime, dioramas, dressing up as a character, creating book jackets, writing a report, or making a mobile or game (see Chapter 6).
- Create small informal reading areas with rugs, pillows, and comfortable chairs. A corner of the room usually works well.
- For students who are not motivated to read, provide short reading assignments and plenty of encouragement.
- Provide examples and simplify directions. Global children *need* examples *before* they understand a rule.
- Simplify complex or confusing directions. This is especially important for globals and for students who are not strongly auditory.
- For strongly global youngsters, de-emphasize reading activities that require highly analytic abilities (missing sounds, words, or letters, crossword puzzles, word searches).
- Provide choices of reading materials, groupings, and places to work.

The first three chapters on reading have described many effective strategies for increasing reading achievement and motivation. Chapter 4 will describe the powerful Continuum of Modeling Reading Methods. This tool can be used by teachers to improve students' reading fluency within *minutes*.

REFERENCES

1. *The Power of Reading Styles* (Syosset, N.Y.: NRSI, 1995). Write for a free copy: NRSI, P.O. Box 737, Syosset, NY 11791, or call 1-800-331-3117. Also see B. L. Skipper, "Reading with Style," *American School Board Journal*, February 1997, pp. 36-37; and A. Snyder, "On the Road to Reading Recovery," *The School Administrator*, vol. 88, 1994, pp. 23-24.
2. For information about the Reading Style Inventory® (RSI) or reading styles training, contact: NRSI, P.O. Box 737, Syosset, NY 11791, or call 1-800-331-3117.
3. L. Barber, M. Carbo, and R. Thomasson, "A Comparative Study of the Reading Styles Program to Extant Programs of Teaching Reading" (Syosset, N.Y.: National Reading Styles Institute, 1996).

National Study

Research in reading styles has demonstrated that the process of assessing and matching students' reading styles results in significant increases on standardized tests of reading achievement.

Larry Barber, director of the Phi Delta Kappa Center on Evaluation, Development, and Research, collaborated with Marie Carbo and Rebecca Thomasson on a national research study that concluded its two-year phase in 1993. Data for the study, which were analyzed by Dr. Barber, were drawn from 10 states, representing urban, inner-city, suburban, and rural students in grades 1-9. The study also examined various ability levels, including students from a school for the severely handicapped.

The multi-site replicated experiment concluded:

> At this time it is defensible to conclude that if the reading styles program is implemented to at least minimum criterion level (85%) and is carried out over a school year, one could expect the children in the reading styles program to obtain consistently higher achievement scores and gains than those children in the extant or control programs.[3]

CHAPTER 4

Achieving High Reading Gains with Modeling Strategies

Jim, Steven, and Maria will not learn to read this year because of wrong instruction. If the proper measures are not taken, they may be condemned to a life of illiteracy. Jim will sit for 30 minutes and stare at a book during sustained silent reading (SSR). Jim's friends across the hall, Steven and Maria, won't fare any better. They will try to read the same book together (paired reading), each of them stumbling and missing words.

By the end of the school year, these three children won't be able to read, won't like to read, and will do poorly on reading tests.

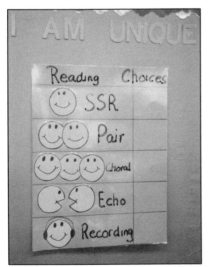

Photo courtesy of Robb Elementary School, Uvalde, Texas.

Children choose their preferred method in Mrs. Dorflinger's class.

Unfortunately, many adults will think that they are kids who "just can't learn to read." A whopping 270 hours of precious instructional time will have been wasted. Continued wrong instruction will put these three young people—and millions like them—at risk of dropping out of school and will severely curtail their job potential for life.

This waste is absolutely preventable. Not a single minute of it has to occur. Each of our three youngsters *can learn* to read easily and very well—if the correct instructional strategies are used.

Hearing and seeing the words before reading aloud helps students to develop reading fluency and self-confidence.

Photo courtesy of Roosevelt Elementary School, Medford, Oregon.

Listening to books recorded at a slightly slow pace enables this student to follow along easily and repeat the recordings as often as needed.

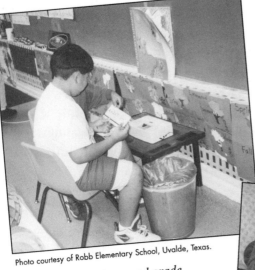

Photo courtesy of Robb Elementary School, Uvalde, Texas.

In Mrs. Guzman's second grade, children can listen to words and phrases recorded by their teacher and then record the material themselves.

Photo courtesy of Roosevelt Elementary School, Medford, Oregon.

Sufficient modeling beforehand allows students to read in pairs with ease and fluency.

In this and the next chapter, we'll look at powerful strategies designed to effect high, rapid reading gains, especially with young people in the bottom third. With these strategies, children like Jim, Steven, and Maria will not only choose high-level books that interest them, but they'll be able to read them, too! And they will make *remarkable* gains in reading.

Too Little Modeling Prevents Success

How can we help Jim, Steven, and Maria quickly? The answer lies in a tool called the Continuum of Modeling Reading Methods[1] (Figure 4.1).

The idea behind the Continuum is a simple yet powerful one. Children who are not yet independent readers, especially those who are reading well below their potential, need frequent modeling of high-interest materials. By modeling, I mean that a competent reader reads aloud high-interest text, *while the less able reader listens to and looks at the words being read.* After several repetitions of this modeling, the learner reads it aloud. If he or she cannot read the passage fluently, a competent reader should provide more modeling while the learner follows along, looking at the words as they are read aloud until the material is mastered. If this process causes the learner too much struggle, then easier material should be used.

Many youngsters simply do not receive the amount and kind of modeling they require; they are pushed along too fast. Children who are barely able to read often spend too much time either in paired reading, where they may listen to reading modeled by another child who cannot read well, or attempting sustained silent reading, trying to do what they're not yet able to do: read independently books that interest them. At a time in their schooling when they desperately need to hear good reading modeled repeatedly *before* they try to read on their own, they don't receive such modeling.

How the Continuum of Modeling Reading Methods Works

There are many different kinds of modeling methods. I've included several of the more popular ones on the Continuum of

FIGURE 4.1

Continuum of Modeling Reading Methods
by Marie Carbo

The goal of the modeling strategies on this continuum is reading alone with ease and enjoyment (SSR). Moving from bottom to top, each strategy requires increasingly more reading independence of the student and less modeling by the teacher. Teachers should select the strategy that is most appropriate for a student or a group. Generally, strategies that provide the most modeling should be used with beginning readers and those who cannot read a particular text with good fluency.

Low Teacher Involvement
High Student Independence

Sustained Silent Reading	Each person in the classroom, including the teacher, reads alone. The time period for a group can range from about 10 to 45 minutes per session. A strong emphasis is placed on self-selection of reading materials and reading for pleasure.
Paired Reading	Two students take turns reading a passage or story. Teachers may pair youngsters of similar or dissimilar reading abilities and/or interests, or children may select partners. An emphasis is usually placed on reading for pleasure.
Choral Reading	Two or more students read a passage in unison. Less able readers try to follow the reading model provided by the more adept readers in the group. Group members may be teachers, parents, students, etc.
Neurological Impress	The teacher sits behind the youngster and reads into the child's ear. Both hold the book and read in unison. The child places his or her finger under the line of print being read by the teacher. The purpose is reading fluency; the teacher asks no comprehension questions (Heckelman, 1969).
Echo Reading	After discussing a passage, the teacher reads it aloud while the student (or group) follows along in the text. Then the teacher reads aloud a small portion, i.e., a sentence or paragraph, and the student reads it back. This procedure continues until the passage is completed.
Recorded Books	The youngster listens one or more times to a word-for-word recording while following along in the text, and then reads it aloud. Less able readers can listen one to three times to two- to five-minute segments recorded at a slower-than-usual pace, and then read the passage aloud. (Carbo, 1989).
Shared Reading	A high-interest book or chart, often enlarged and containing many pictures and predictable language, is placed in front of students. The teacher reads the story while pointing to the words and pausing to ask questions. After a few readings, youngsters are encouraged to read along with the teacher.
High Teacher Involvement **Low Student Independence**	©Copyright Marie Carbo, 1993.

Modeling Reading Methods. Those methods that provide the most modeling of a text before the student reads it independently are at the *bottom* of the Continuum. At the very top of the Continuum, is our goal: sustained silent reading (SST). During SST the student receives no modeling of the text. What is modeled by the teacher and other students is the actual act of reading alone silently.

"Emerging readers need frequent modeling of high-interest materials."

Now it's easy to understand why Jim, Steven, and Maria are not succeeding. They've been pushed upward on the Continuum too fast—like baby birds pushed to fly before their wings are strong enough. Jim, Steven, and Maria are simply not yet ready to fly— either together (paired reading) or solo (sustained silent reading).

Since Jim, Steven, and Maria don't read well, they need a great deal of modeling. They need to have many experiences with the methods toward the *bottom* of the Continuum (shared reading, recorded books, echo reading). This modeling will strengthen their oral language, sight vocabulary, and reading fluency. As their reading improves and they become more competent and confident, they'll be ready to practice reading with the help of good readers (neurological impress, choral reading, paired reading). Finally, they'll be able to spend more and more of their time reading alone. The Continuum will show you how to make this happen.

How to Use the Continuum

In general, provide less able readers with many opportunities to hear and see good reading being modeled. Good models of reading are particularly important for youngsters who need a great deal of repetition—especially those with low English proficiency. For these children, spend more time using the methods at the lower end of the Continuum. In these early stages of literacy, it is also helpful to read aloud some stories written by the children themselves. As the

47

youngsters' reading fluency improves, move up the Continuum and use those methods that provide less and less modeling. Students who are independent readers should spend more of their reading time at the upper end of the Continuum.

Amount and Kind of Modeling Provided

Photo courtesy of Sacred Heart Academy, Hempstead, New York.

After experiencing sufficient modeling with recordings, these two boys take turns reading to each other.

Let's look at the amount and kind of modeling provided by each of the methods on the Continuum, starting with the bottom method and moving to the top.

Storytelling and Reading Aloud. These modeling methods are not on the Continuum. If they were, they would be placed just below shared reading.

Storytelling models oral language through stories Reading aloud familiarizes children with the sound and sense of written language.[2]

Shared Reading: Children hear a story being read and look at the words as the reader traces his/her finger or a pointer below the words. Children are encouraged, but not expected, to read the story back. The major purposes of this method are to motivate students to read, to help them understand that writing proceeds from left to right, and to connect written and spoken language. This is all done in a relaxed setting, with a great deal of repetition for those youngsters who need it.[3]

Photo courtesy of Wendy Hill, Twin Ridges Elementary School, N. San Juan, California.

It's hard to resist glancing over to a friend's book during sustained silent reading—when the book looks so interesting.

Recorded Books: Children see and hear a passage or story being read to them. They are expected to read the passage or story back. Both commercially recorded books and teacher-recorded books can be used for this method. I recommend a special method of recording that I developed especially for struggling readers (see Chapter 5).[4]

Echo Reading: Usually students hear a live model of a small portion of a passage and immediately read it back. The text might be a sentence, a paragraph, or a longer amount of material. This method is one step up from recorded books because the children usually hear the modeled reading only once.

Choral Reading: Two or more students read a passage in unison.

Photo courtesy of Mike Kasnic, Butcher Children's School, Emporia, Kansas.

Shared reading: A friend reads a story to his buddy.

Choral reading can include a variety of people (including the teacher) reading together. The passage can be very short or quite lengthy. In this method, the less proficient reader must try to read along with the model as it is being provided. Choral reading is more difficult than the previous methods because the student is expected to read a passage at the same time that others are reading it. No previous modeling need have occurred.[5]

Paired Reading: Two students take turns reading one or more passages. In addition to simply alternating passages, one student may act as the narrator while the other is a character in the story; any number of variations are possible. Notice that with this method each student is expected to read some parts of a text independently. Since each student reads a different part of the text, no exact model is provided before the reading. Some general modeling of reading may occur if at least one member of the pair is a good reader.

Sustained Silent Reading: Each child reads alone for a set period of time. SSR is the goal of the Continuum (see Figure 4.1).

Be Creative!

Use the Continuum of Modeling Reading Methods in creative ways. Combine modeling methods when it makes sense to do so. For example, before children choral-read a passage, they might listen to a tape recording of it to improve their fluency. Or a teacher might do an echo reading session with a small group, having the group members choral-read a passage back after it is modeled. The list of variations is endless.

Try to place your students in experiences that will assure their success. Whenever you see them struggling, refer to the Continuum for help. Remember that all the methods on the Continuum provide practice in reading, but some of the methods also provide modeling. Children need to spend the most time with the method or methods that will help them attain reading fluency.

Learning to read should be easy and it should feel like fun. Providing the right kind of modeling method at the right time helps a child to improve fluency, word recognition, and confidence. It also improves comprehension. When a young person can read words easily, and when he or she feels good about being able to read, then that child's mind is freed to *understand* what is being read. There's the goal of reading.

Photo courtesy of Jan Sutherlin Lane, Glynn County Schools, Brunswick, Georgia.

Students listen to a friend read aloud in a perfect setting.

Recommendations for Principals

• Become familiar with the Continuum of Modeling Reading Methods. It could become the focus of your classroom reading visits. Usually, the time frame required is short, and the strategies on the lower levels lend themselves to whole-group instruction.

- Encourage teachers to share ideas for using the Continuum in their classrooms, such as the use of charts with nursery rhymes or poems on overheads. Emphasize the need for students to *see the words as they are read aloud.*
- Have a group of your teachers train volunteers to work with students who are at various stages of the Continuum.
- Plan a parent group-training session to assist parents with using the Continuum with their students at home. If the parents are non-readers, provide taped stories to send home with the student. Ask the parents to listen to the taped book with their child and follow along in the book.

Recommendations for Teachers

- Try replacing periods of sustained silent reading with specific time for the Continuum of Modeling Reading Methods. Each student can practice his or her reading by using a method on the Continuum that is beneficial.
- For inclusion students and those for whom English is a second language, increase fluency, word recognition, and vocabulary by using the strategies at the bottom of the continuum often, such as shared reading, the Carbo Recorded-Book® Method, and echo reading.
- Place the students described above strategically in small groups when choral reading is taking place. If they have had opportunities for practice beforehand, especially with a recording of the passage, they are likely to participate to some degree. The benefit to their self-esteem is often substantial, as these youngsters are included in groups and are able to read some of the words.
- Remember to use the Continuum of Modeling Reading Methods with content reading areas such as math word problems, social studies, and science.

In Chapter 5 we will look carefully at what we have found to be one of the most important reading methods on the Continuum of Modeling Reading Methods—the Carbo Recorded-Book® Method. This method has resulted in exceptionally high gains in reading comprehension and fluency in very short periods of time.

REFERENCES

1. M. Carbo, "Selecting the 'Right' Reading Method," *Teaching K-8,* vol. 27, 1996, pp. 84-87.

2. J. Trelease, *The Read-Aloud Handbook* (New York: Penguin, 1992).

3. D. Holdaway, "Shared Book Experience: Teaching Reading Using Favorite Books," *Theory Into Practice,* vol. 21, 1982, pp. 293-300.

4. M. Carbo, *How to Record Books for Maximum Reading Gains* (Syosset, N.Y.: NRSI, 1989).

5. J.K. McCauley and D.S. McCauley, "Using Choral Reading to Promote Language Learning for ESL Students," *The Reading Teacher,* vol. 45, 1992, pp. 526-33.

CHAPTER 5

Achieving High Reading Gains with Recorded Books

Within minutes, Tommy was reading a book three years above his reading level. He had worked for only 10 minutes with a special recording of his book. After only six weeks, Tommy gained an incredible 1.3 years in reading!

What's the secret of these remarkably effective recordings? I had observed that my severely handicapped students enjoyed commercially recorded books, but they couldn't keep up with the fast pace of the recordings. I decided to record somewhat challenging, high-interest books at a slightly slower pace, recording just a few minutes of text on each tape side. The children would listen to my special recordings a few times and follow along in their books. Then miracles seemed to happen. They all began to read much more smoothly and confidently, and they improved dramatically in reading fluency and comprehension.

Photo courtesy of Roosevelt Elementary School, Medford, Oregon.

First-graders enjoy a recorded book.

That was more than 20 years ago. Now tens of thousands of teachers have learned the Carbo Recorded-Book® Method, and many have told us their amazing success stories. Best of all, this method has helped teachers accomplish the goals of this book: to raise reading abilities and test scores and to nurture in children a love of reading.

What It Is and How It Works

For many young children and poor readers, there's a substantial time lag between when they see and say a word. That lag produces slow, laborious reading that makes comprehension all but impossible. It's terribly difficult for students to recall what a passage is about when they have to spend so much effort figuring out each word. In effect, the recording does what the child is not yet able to do naturally: It verbalizes the printed words with the correct pace, phrasing, and expression. As a result, students make fewer reading errors, and the possibility of forming incorrect reading patterns is diminished.

Best of all, it's not necessary to record dull, simple reading materials to develop a student's sight vocabulary. (In fact, words presented within high-interest contexts tend to be easier to learn and retain than words presented in isolation or within a dull context.) Since each student can decide the number of times to listen to a recording and when to read aloud, the child is in control of his or her own learning.

> "The recording does what the child is not yet able to do naturally: It verbalizes the printed words with the correct pace, phrasing, and expression."

Formula for Success

To be most effective, recorded books should be above the student's reading level and close to, or even slightly higher than, his or her language-comprehension level. The simple key is this: If the gap between the student's reading level and the level of the book is small, record about five minutes of a story on one tape side at a fairly normal pace, with natural expression and phrasing. If the gap is large, use a slower pace and fewer words to a phrase, exaggerate your expression, and record much less on a tape side—only about two minutes instead of five.[1]

> "Record at a fairly slow pace to enable your students to absorb the words they see and hear."

Carbo Recorded-Book® Method

Samples of recorded books are available from the National Reading Styles Institute (800-331-3117). These recordings provide models for teachers to imitate. To make your own recordings, here are my three golden rules:

Photo courtesy of Howard County Schools, Maryland.

A young boy relaxes with a good book well above his reading level. The recording will enable him to read it back fluently.

1. Books should be recorded in very small segments, because most young-sters will need to listen to a tape side more than once to be able to read the portion back fluently. That's why only about one to five minutes should be recorded on each tape side. Therefore, a 15-page storybook might require four tape sides, while a longer book might take as many as 10.

2. Record at a fairly slow pace to enable your students to absorb the words they see and hear. The short, natural phrases translate the printed page into meaningful segments. The pauses are crucial; they allow the brain to take in and sort the text, and they help to increase both comprehension and word recognition.

3. Record with good expression; that, too, aids memory. Research indicates that speech stimuli—such as moaning, coughing, crying, and laughing—and the melody or inflection of the voice stimulate the right hemisphere of the brain and increase retention.

How to Record: Step by Step

1. Set aside a block of quiet time for recording.
2. Decide what book to record and code the tapes accordingly.
3. Speak into the microphone from a distance of about eight inches.
4. In general, use the same naturally expressive voice you'd use if you were reading to a single child.
5. Convey your interest in the book through your voice. Let the child *feel* your enthusiasm.
6. Begin by reading the story title, pausing, then telling the page to which the reader should turn. Always pause long enough so the youngster has ample time to turn pages and look at pictures.
7. End each tape so that you draw to a close that portion of the story. Example: "Brian is very sad now. On the next tape side we'll find out why." Then pause and say, "That ends this recording."

> "Convey your interest in the book through your voice. Let the child feel your enthusiasm."

---

8. Tell the student when to turn the page. As you begin each story, say, "Turn to page __." Slowly reduce the cues until you need only pause, state the page number, and pause again. It's important to work up to omitting the words. "Turn to page...," because this interruption tends to distract the listener.
9. Since the story is all-important, your voice should be softer when giving cues to the student than it is when you're reading.
10. Your phrasing is very important. Read the story in logical sections. The way you phrase helps youngsters understand the passage and increases their comprehension.

11. If you think a word may be unfamiliar to students, give it space by pausing slightly before and after it. That will give youngsters more time to look at it, absorb it, and retain it.

Photo courtesy of Howard County Schools, Maryland.

Donna Michel's class prepares to use the listening center with their taped recordings.

12. Read slowly so that students can visually track the words they hear, but not so slowly that they become bored or comprehension is lost.

"Select books to record based on the interests of your students."

---

13. Teach students with visual perception problems (who may lose their place on the page easily) to follow the recording by placing a finger under the words they hear. Show them how to use an index card to keep their place.

14. Use the child's own writing. For emerging readers, it often helps to combine the child's own writing with the Recorded-Book® Method. Most youngsters can more easily recall their own written language rather than the language in a storybook, which may sound unfamiliar to the child.

    Encourage the child to dictate or write a simple story. Then record it and have the child listen to the recording a few times while following along in the story. Do this for several stories. Then slowly transition the youngster to recordings of books.

How to Select Books

When you're recording books for a youngster, consider these four factors: 1) the quality of the writing; and the student's 2) interest level; 3) language-comprehension level; and 4) reading level.

Quality of the Writing. To select well-written children's books, your school librarian (and also lists of award-winning books) can be helpful. If a book seems interesting, read a portion and check to see if the author uses imaginative language, if the book has a clear purpose, and if it captures the reader's interest right away.

Student Interest. Select books to record based on the interests of your students. As soon as they begin to listen to recorded books, their word retention improves dramatically in *direct proportion* to their interest in the book. After they develop an initial sight vocabulary, students of all ages make the most rapid gains with books close to their *language-comprehension, level,* which usually is above their reading level.

Photo courtesy of Lake Washington S.D., Washington.

Students listen to a recording of a story before meeting with their reading group.

Language Comprehension and Reading Levels. Most young children and poor readers are assigned so-called "high-interest," low-readability materials. Seldom is the student's language-comprehension level considered, although it's a powerful factor. Select books to record that at least approach the child's spoken language ability.

For example, suppose you were choosing books to record for two average youngsters: Jermaine, a fourth-grader, and Thomas, in the sixth grade. Both youngsters read on a third-grade level. You would select a more difficult book for Thomas because he's interested in, and capable of understanding, sixth-grade vocabulary and concepts.

To judge whether you've chosen a book of the appropriate level for a youngster, use these rules of thumb:

- Students should not be able to read a book fluently before listening to the recording.
- After two or three listenings to a book recording, students should be able to read the passage back smoothly, with no more than two or three errors. They should also be able to provide an oral summary and answer comprehension questions.

There are many variations on the Recorded-Book® Method, depending on the needs of the group. Teachers can record for an individual child or an entire class. Recordings can be made in any language, and even more than one language can be used on a tape side.

At Margil Elementary School in San Antonio, for example, teachers recorded some books' introductions in Spanish and then continued by recording the entire story in English. The possibilities are as endless as the imaginations of those who work with children.

Recommendations for Principals

The building principal can use the Carbo Recorded-Book® Method to create a highly effective reading program that provides enormous benefits to children. Our research indicates that this method produces re-markable gains when

Photo courtesy of Barbara Hinds, Bob Hope Elementary School, San Antonio, Texas.

Two buddies listen to their recorded books sitting side by side.

there are ample books recorded, when the method is used with at-risk readers at least four days per week, and when the books and recordings are accessible and used in a structured manner.

How to Get Started

A good way to bring the Carbo Recorded-Book® Method into your building is to share this chapter with several teachers. Ask the teachers to try the method with just one child—preferably a child reading below grade level who's not making much progress in reading.

After a week or so, discuss the results with those teachers. Even though their tape

Children choose from the color-coded recorded books right above their workplace.

recordings may not be perfectly correct, the chances are still very good that they will have seen positive changes in the reading ability of the children using the tapes. Those initial successes can be so profound that teachers will want to experiment further with the recordings and include more of their at-risk readers. Share the successes of this first group with a wider circle of teachers, and begin to expand and organize the program. Next, secure samples of recorded books to share with teachers (see "Resources" at the end of this chapter).

"Teachers can record for an individual child or an entire class. Recordings can be made in any language, and even more than one language can be used on a tape side."

A Dozen Recommendations for Principals

Here are 12 recommendations for starting and developing a highly effective program of recorded books—one that can raise the reading levels of your students very quickly.

1. Secure permission from copyright holders to record books.
2. Have on hand these basic materials:
   - quality tape recorders with microphones;
   - tape players and headsets for the children;

- blank tapes (no more than 15 minutes per tape side);
- high-interest books for recording;
- fine-tipped, indelible marking pens for coding the tapes; and
- plastic hanging bags for storing the books and tapes.

3. Try to provide time for your teachers to record. Encourage and support their efforts.

4. Try to schedule brief weekly meetings for teachers to share their successes, observations, and materials.

5. As the need arises, purchase books based on children's interests.

6. Provide teachers who use the method extensively with book shelving and storage for the tapes.

7. Schedule a short period of time each week when children can read to you to "show off" their progress in reading.

8. Schedule older children and volunteers to listen to children read. Volunteers can also help code and organize the tapes.

9. Train talented children and volunteers to record the tapes. This training should be done by the teachers who have become highly competent with the method.

10. Store master copies of all tapes. Make sure there are sufficient copies of the books. Sometimes paperbacks go out of print.

11. Provide extra copies of some taped books so that children can borrow them to demonstrate their improved reading abilities to parents or guardians.

12. Finally, buy extra copies of your most popular books; they'll become well worn by your formerly at-risk readers!

Photo courtesy of Robb Elementary School, Uvalde, Texas.

In Lilian Flores' fourth-grade bilingual class, students listen to recordings to improve their reading and to accelerate the learning of English.

Recommendations for Teachers

- Take the time to instruct each student in the proper care and use of the tape recorder. Model the procedure for them, and then have them model for you. The extra time this takes in the beginning will be time well-spent.
- Include in your lesson plans the read-back portion of the Carbo Recorded-Book® Method. It is most important.
- If other persons have made the recordings, be sure to check and determine if the recording is a good model for the student.
- Remember that the choice and interest of the student is more important than the teacher's choice or preference.
- Keep simple records of what the student is reading and how he or she is progressing. You might staple a list of the books on one side of a folder and a sheet for date, book title, and comments on another. When listening to a student read, jot down notes describing the number of repetitions needed, quality of the students' read-back and summary, and the youngster's ability to answer a few comprehension questions.
- Develop a type of record-keeping that allows you to track the reading growth of the student. An "oral" portfolio is an excellent method. Using a 60- or 90-minute tape for each child, have the student read a self-selected paragraph into the tape recorder on a weekly basis. Before each reading, either the student or you should say the day's date. The student (and their parents) will be amazed to hear the oral reading improvement over a period of time.
- If volunteers or instructional aides are conducting the read-back segment, be sure to train them in the record-keeping aspect of the read-back.

In Chapter 6, I'll discuss strategies for the preparation of hands-on materials that can improve reading skills. Elementary children (especially underachievers) often are strongly tactile/kinesthetic; their learning is greatly enhanced by the involvement of their hands and their bodies. I'll also focus on how to elicit the assistance of volunteers to create materials for teachers, and what materials and space are needed for volunteers to work in school buildings.

Resources

Books that have been recorded with the method described in this chapter are available from: NRSI, P.O. Box 737, Syosset, NY 11791. Ph. 800-331-3117.

REFERENCES

1. See the following by Marie Carbo: *How to Record Books for Maximum Reading Gains* (Syosset, N.Y.: National Reading Styles Institute, 1989); "Advanced Book Recording: Turning It Around for Poor Readers," *Early Years*, vol. 15, 1985, pp. 46-48; and "Eliminating the Need for Dumbed-Down Textbooks," *Educational Horizons,* vol. 70, 1992, pp. 189-93.

Many elementary-aged students are strongly tactile and kinesthetic.

Photo courtesy of Jim Hill Middle School, Minot, North Dakota.

These students search for answers to sentences and then line up the statements in correct order.

Photo courtesy of Jim Hill Middle School, Minot, North Dakota.

It's more fun to match synonyms with a set of self-checking task cards.

CHAPTER 6

Achieving Higher Reading Gains with Active Learning

You pass by a classroom and see the children all busily engaged in activity. There's movement of one kind or another everywhere you look. But are they *learning*? Are the activities you see linked to important objectives, and has the teacher established sufficient structure and routine so that materials and resources are efficiently used?

Active learning, *done well*, can substantially increase students' motivation and skill development. Ample research supports this statement. On the other hand, there is little or no research to support the current widespread use of worksheets.

Photo courtesy of Stemley Road Elementary School, Talladega, Alabama.

Teachers at Stemley Road Elementary School created this laminated hopscotch game for practicing reading skills.

Teachers can accelerate the learning of needed reading skills by accommodating students' reading style strengths. Young children and underachievers need many small-group experiences that make learning fun and interesting, and that allow them to touch, feel, move, and experience as they learn. Active learning satisfies these reading style needs and helps children become motivated, competent readers.

Active Learning vs. Traditional Teaching

Most learning in the very early years of childhood is a result of touching, feeling, moving, and experiencing. Indeed, many children don't become strongly visual until after third grade and strongly auditory until fifth grade.[1] Boys begin school more strongly tactile and kinesthetic than girls and remain so throughout the primary grades. Boys also consistently outnumber girls in remedial reading classes by about four or five to one.

The reading styles of both young children and underachievers show clearly that activity-based experiences are imperative—but American students still do about 1,000 reading worksheets each school year! And each school year they become more and more turned off to reading, according to the National Assessment of Educational Progress (NAEP), which reports that library use and reading motivation and comprehension have declined steadily for over a decade. The NAEP has strongly advised a sharp reduction in the number of worksheets used to teach reading (NAEP, 1994).

"Active learning, done well,
can substantially increase students'
motivation and skill development."

But worksheets aren't the only problem. John Goodlad's classic study of the behavior of U.S. students and teachers in classrooms nationwide revealed that the predominant instructional style is frontal teaching: In most classrooms, the teacher is active and the students are passive. Teachers lecture, write on the board, and work with groups. Students, for the most part, are expected to listen and watch—and to do worksheets.

Clearly, to teach reading skills well and to increase student motivation, we must accommodate the styles of young children and underachievers through a decreased use of worksheets and teacher lecture and an increased use of active learning.

CHECKLIST FOR LEVELS OF ACTIVE LEARNING

Not all active learning activities require a lot of preparation. Think of active learning strategies in three categories, each requiring increased levels of teacher preparation. Encourage teachers to use at least Level 1 strategies and then move on to Levels 2 and 3, which provide greater amounts of activity for the learner.

Level 1: Activity Separate from Learning

This lowest level provides little or no activity *during* learning but can relieve the tedium caused by sitting at a desk for most of the day. Movement serves to refresh youngsters physically and enables them to concentrate better on listening and pencil-and-paper tasks.

Photo courtesy of Roosevelt Elementary School, Medford, Oregon.

Allowing for mobility, this sixth-grader works at the overhead projector.

Examples:

Allow children to:

- Stand at their desks while doing worksheets or similar activities.
- Move to centers to get worksheets or needed materials.
- Go to the class library for a book, or to a center to work.
- Sit in carpeted areas to work.
- Sharpen their pencils, get a drink of water, or sign out to the bathroom as needed.
- Have jobs that allow some mobility (open/close windows, distribute/collect papers, run errands).
- Clean out their desks or parts of the classroom.

Level 2: Simulated Experiences

A simulated experience often involves the child kinesthetically (whole-body movement) and usually does not require much in the way of materials and preparation.[2] These activities can be done with an entire class, but are more often appropriate for small groups.

By pantomiming the word "swimming," this kinesthetic young boy is more likely to remember the word.

Examples:

- Children pantomime parts of a story or an answer to a question and then describe their pantomime orally or in writing.
- Children role-play characters and events from a story, or role-play an answer to a question.
- In groups, children create movements to describe poetry as a narrator reads.
- As a word is said, children clap once for each syllable. Variations: snap fingers, stamp feet, take steps, hop.

- Children write a compound word on a card and then cut it in half. The teacher mixes and distributes the halves. Then each child finds the classmate with the matching word half. Each pair acts out its word.

> "Games can provide multisensory learning experiences that capitalize on students' perceptual strengths."

Level 3: Games

Games can provide multisensory learning experiences that capitalize on students' perceptual strengths. Games can heighten interest in books and reading, improve skills, and allow structured peer interactions. The first two items below are "gamelike" and require less preparation than the following ones. Examples:

- Each student is given a "yes" card and a "no" card. Cards are held up to answer questions posed by the teacher or by another child.

*Card games,
electroboards, and
task cards can be
used to teach specific
reading skills*

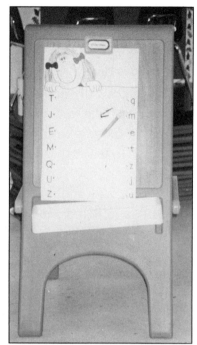

*This electroboard on an easel is
for standing/playing in Nancy
Aleman's kindergarten classroom.*

*Two friends practice
their reading skills
with a game of
concentration.
They're developing
memory and social
skills, too!*

*Pairs of students challenge each other to select the
word being defined.*

(This technique becomes self-checking when the children look at one another's answers.)

- Reading Jeopardy. Answers to reading questions are placed on cards. Two lines of students are formed, much like a spelling bee. Members of each team compete to provide the correct question for each answer.
- Card games, electroboards, board games, and task cards can be used to teach specific reading skills. When starting, it's advisable to use a few standard formats and to cut and paste ideas from workbooks and other commercial sources.
- Bulletin board games are excellent for kinesthetic learners since they use the larger muscle groups. Simply make a large game and staple it to the bulletin board (e.g., large electroboards, pockets with cards to sort).
- Enlarged game boards can be made using shower curtains. These become "floor games," which are excellent for kinesthetic learners.

Special Note About Games

In general, modeling reading methods should precede skill work. Children should be able to read words fluently in context *before* those words and phrases are placed in games. After children can read a book fluently, then use hands-on materials to practice words and phrases from the story and to improve comprehension skills.

Recommendations for Principals

Principals can encourage large amounts of active learning targeted to specific reading skills. Think of active learning on a continuum, and guide your teachers increasingly toward Levels 2 and 3.

To help teachers adopt more and more Level 3 strategies (games), it's important to provide them with planning time, guidance, needed materials, places to work, volunteers to help, and management strategies. Here are some suggestions for getting started:

- Begin by evaluating the level of active learning in your school. You might use the Levels of Active Learning checklist.
- On classroom visits, ask teachers which objective they are teaching with a particular activity. If the activity has been planned as part of the instructional process, the teacher should be able to

identify the activity's purpose. Also, ask the students to explain what they are doing. If the objectives have been identified by the teacher, the students should be able to explain why they are participating in the activity.

- Accumulate a library of books with game patterns and teaching suggestions, such as those listed in the references at the end of this chapter.
- Maintain a list of volunteers to help create hands-on materials. Volunteers may be parents, students, former teachers, the elderly—anyone with the interest and time. (Note: You may want to schedule volunteers for only one or two work sessions at first. For long-term work, select those who are easiest to work with.)
- Discuss the benefits of active learning with your teachers and ask them to use the checklist to self-evaluate their classrooms. They may add items to the three levels and count strategies they use that are similar to the ones listed.

"Team planning and effort are necessary to enable active learning to become a strong part of the strategies used in your building."

- Identify a core group of teachers, or work with the entire faculty to create games. Try various kinesthetic strategies. (Explain that volunteers will do most of the work.)
- Accumulate such basic materials as construction and contact paper, colored 5"x8" cards, permanent markers of various sizes and colors, envelopes and small boxes for storage, card pockets (like the ones used in library cards), and, if at all possible, a laminating machine. Ask your teachers for suggestions.
- Designate a working place and a scheduled meeting time for planning activities and games. A permanent room where materials can be stored is ideal.
- Decide on the objectives to be taught. Evaluate with staff the objectives suggested by curriculum guides, sample tests, and worksheets. Emphasize the importance of targeting specific skills needed by your students.

- Ask a core group of teachers to create a prototype of several types of games that can then be copied by volunteers (i.e., task cards, electroboards, board games). Commercial examples of game formats should be available as guides, as well as game books such as *Patterns for Hands-On Learning.*[3]
- Have a core group of teachers begin by designing paper games that teach specific reading skills. (Request free articles that show teachers how to do this from NRSI, P.O. Box 737, Syosset, NY 11791. Include a stamped, self-addressed large envelope.)
- Schedule volunteers regularly to create the hands-on materials designed by your teachers. Provide the volunteers with the necessary materials (and a laminating machine nearby), prototypes of each game, and the teacher's detailed description. Example: "Make an electroboard with these lists of adjectives and character names. Label it *Pinkerton, Behave!*"
- Some teachers are natural managers and organizers. Meet regularly with teachers so that they can share their ideas on classroom management.
- Finally, encourage teachers to visit one another's classrooms to learn management and organizational ideas, as well as teaching strategies. Try teaming global and analytic teachers to share ideas.

Recommendations for Teachers

- Use creative ways to help children to remember words. Janet Martin's new book, *Sight Words That Stick,*[4] is ideal!
- Before the class begins work in each new activity or center, model and demonstrate the proper use of the activity. Ask for suggestions from students.
- Have the class assist in setting up guidelines for proper behavior. (They usually set much stricter guidelines than teachers would.)
- Move slowly when beginning activities and establishing new levels of student independence within your classroom. Establish, rehearse, and reward proper behaviors. Take time to explain the rules and discuss why they are needed.

- Students can assist in creating activities. Be prepared to accept game pieces and materials that are somewhat imperfect in appearance.
- Work closely with the art teacher, the physical education teacher, and the computer lab technician (if your school has one). These subject-area teachers often can help to provide activities or game formats.

Team planning and effort are necessary to enable active learning to become a strong part of the strategies used in your building. Remember that young children and underachievers tend to have strongly global, tactile, and kinesthetic reading styles. Active learning capitalizes on these styles. The resulting increase in student motivation and the acceleration of learning are well worth the effort involved.

But it's possible to improve the reading ability of students and still see little improvement in test scores. Therefore, Chapter 8 focuses on raising reading scores. It emphasizes the use of reading styles strategies and item analysis and describes some of the best ways to improve students' test-taking skills.

REFERENCES

1. R. Restak, *The Brain: The Last Frontier* (New York: Doubleday, 1979).

2. A. Gilbert, *Teaching the Three Rs* (Englewood Cliffs, N.J.: Prentice Hall, 1977).

3. R. Thomasson, *Patterns for Hands-On Learning* (Syosset, N.Y.: National Reading Styles Institute, 1993); P. Kaye, *Games for Reading* (New York: Pantheon Books, 1984).

4. J. Martin, *Sight Words That Stick* (Syosset, N.Y.: National Reading Styles Institute, 1996).

Well-organized, relaxing, and inviting, these classroom environments help students with special needs to develop independence, self-confidence, and needed academic skills.

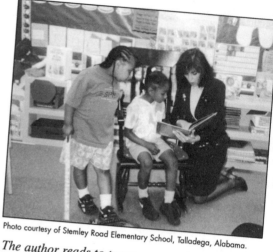

Photo courtesy of Stemley Road Elementary School, Talladega, Alabama.

The author reads to two youngsters in an ideal classroom setting that invites children to enjoy learning to read.

Photo courtesy of Bob Hope Elementary School, San Antonio, Texas.

Ah! A mural of calming water, low light, lots of recorded books, and a comfortable, cushioned chair. Sheer heaven and a great place to learn to read.

Photo courtesy of Stemley Road Elementary School, Talladega, Alabama.

A beautifully organized recorded-book system at Stemley Road Elementary contains a series of listening centers. Each is color-coded by reading level. The Book of the Week is read by all.

CHAPTER 7

Accommodating Special Needs Students

Sweeping societal changes in the U.S. are making themselves felt in our schools, particularly in the increased numbers of special needs students. Today's teachers see drug babies, babies born out of wedlock, a growing number of single-parent families, poor and abused youngsters, and children with limited experiences and abilities in English.

Special needs students are often the youngsters who are least likely to be served well within traditional classroom structures. Some have difficulty processing information, some fidget and are highly distractible, some are brilliant and easily bored, some are learning to speak English, and others have emotions and past experiences that make learning difficult. Whether we label these children learning disabled, AD/HD, gifted, bilingual, or emotionally disturbed, they are students who need reading instruction that accommodates their strengths and interests, thereby giving them the best opportunity for success.

Special Thanks...
for their excellent contributions to the following sections:
Beverly Crotts - Accommodating AD/HD and Behaviorally/Emotionally Challenged Children
Cynthia Hernandez - Accommodating Bilingual/LEP Children
Rebecca Thomasson - Accommodating Gifted Children

HOW TO ACCOMMODATE
SPECIAL NEEDS CHILDREN

Recent policies of inclusion have placed many more special needs youngsters within regular classrooms. More than ever before, educators need to be able to recognize and understand the reading styles of each child. They need a wide variety of strategies; they need to know when and how to adapt instruction to their students' needs; and they need adequate staff development, modeling, and coaching so that they become confident in fitting the most effective strategies for particular students.

Research indicates that one of the best ways to accommodate special needs children is to make it a priority to accommodate every child's strengths and needs. This book provides many helpful strategies. The suggestions that follow are specifically designed to accommodate special needs children as they learn to read.

General Recommendations for Principals

• Provide materials and equipment needed by teachers, such as the Reading Style Inventory®, card readers, typewriters, computers, recorded books, tape recorders, high-interest books, and games.
• Make helpful resources available to teachers. See examples listed under "References" at the end of this chapter.
• Encourage the accommodation of students' needs during instruction. For example, if needed, allow the use of colored overlays, mobility, snacks, or music. Also, submit a request to the appropriate testing personnel for permission to use these accommodations during testing.
• Set aside time for teachers and students to share their successes and problems with you and with each other.
• Administer the RSI to your staff and discuss the results, especially in their global and analytic abilities and in perception. Note the large differences in the strengths and weaknesses among your staff, and discuss how those differences affect their learning and teaching. Note that students also display large differences that need to be accommodated instructionally.

- Provide time and funds for teacher training, team building, and planning.
- Encourage cross-age and cross-grade tutoring. Organize parents and other volunteers to help in the school.
- Have a working knowledge and an understanding of ways to accommodate different reading styles.
- Inform parents by letter or in groups of the different activities and behaviors they are likely to see in a reading styles classroom, compared to a traditional classroom.
- Validate movement in the classroom (children moving to centers, playing games).
- Be a resource to your teachers. Stay current with research and be aware of a variety of instructional strategies.
- Share articles related to the concepts and strategies in this book. Encourage staff to do the same.

"Whether we label these children learning disabled, AD/HD, gifted, bilingual, or emotionally disturbed, they are students who need reading instruction that accommodates their strengths and interests, thereby giving them the best opportunity for success."

General Recommendations for Teachers

- Identify students' strengths and appropriate teaching strategies with the Reading Style Inventory®.
- Use reading materials that interest and challenge children. Eliminate boring or inappropriate worksheets and stories.
- Learn a variety of reading methods so that you are able to adapt your instruction as necessary.
- Accommodate students' mobility needs with informal reading areas and centers in your classroom.
- Use peer tutors and volunteers. As appropriate, encourage special needs students to tutor other students.

- Allow youngsters to demonstrate what they have learned in a variety of ways (see Figure 7.1).
- Touching and experiencing are important for many special needs children. Teach with games often and include activities that provide large-muscle movement (drama, pantomime, floor games).

ACCOMMODATING STUDENTS WITH LEARNING DISABILITIES

Youngsters with learning disabilities are often underachievers who have difficulty receiving, sorting, processing, comprehending, and/or producing information. The primary cause of these difficulties is neither an emotional problem nor a lack of language or intelligence. In fact, youngsters with learning disabilities may be exceptionally bright but unable to read simple words or recall math facts. Some brilliant people have had this affliction, including Albert Einstein, Nelson Rockefeller, and Thomas Edison.

To succeed, the learning disabled must learn through their strongest modalities. These children often have dramatic perceptual strengths and weaknesses. Some are strongly visual but not auditory; for others, the reverse is true. And some have neither visual nor auditory strengths.

> "Youngsters with learning disabilities may be exceptionally bright but unable to read simple words or recall math facts."

A child with a learning disability may receive distorted information, such as reversed letters. He or she may have expressive problems; the youngster might receive information accurately but have difficulty demonstrating or expressing it—even though the information has been correctly received and understood. Since many of these youngsters experience repeated failure, they may be greatly stressed, unmotivated, and/or afraid to try.

Recommendations for Principals

- Provide consistent structure and routine in your building. Interrupt classroom schedules as little as possible.
- Ask the learning disabilities specialist in your school or district to share effective strategies with classroom teachers, either at a formal building meeting or as a team-teaching strategy.
- Encourage teachers to share effective strategies that have worked with particular types of special needs students. Be sure to share any materials that are needed.

FIGURE 7.1

Product List

This list of ways to demonstrate knowledge can be expanded over time. Encourage students to explore a variety of ways to share information learned.

Make a travel poster	Write a song
Do a puppet show	Make a time line
Write a letter	Make a video tape
Develop and distribute a questionnaire	Make a list
Plan a journey	Create a slide show
Design and construct a new product	Produce a film
Create a model	Make a collage
Write and produce a play	Collect pictures
Keep a diary	Write an essay
Have a panel discussion	Make a Learning Center
Give a demonstration	Prepare and serve food
Create a slogan or bumper sticker	Design and make costumes
Make a game	Make a tape recording
Create a slide show	Write an autobiography
Hold a press conference	Develop a display
Write a book	Conduct an interview
Create a recipe	Write an essay
Draw a graph	Hold a press conference
Make a mobile	Make a dictionary
Create a musical instrument	Teach a lesson
Design needlework, latch hook	Pantomime

Learning reading skills through movement helps many students learn and retain information more easily.

Photo courtesy Bob Hope Elementary School, San Antonio, Texas.

This youngster stands and stretches (kinesthetic stimulation) to trace over the raised letters of a word, and then writes the word on the board (tactile stimulation). The activity is fun and it promotes learning.

Photo courtesy of Bob Hope Elementary School, San Antonio, Texas.

Four students relax quietly near one another with a variety of activities that include reading with a colored overlay, writing, and reading with a tape.

- Keep a running list of breakthroughs for students. Continually analyze patterns to determine what occurred and why.
- Ask the staff to share their own personal disabilities and compensation strategies.

Recommendations for Teachers

- Provide high levels of structure as needed. Post daily schedules and directions; discuss short- and long-term goals with students; organize materials; post clear, simple directions.
- For students with weak visual skills, place various colored overlays on a page of print. Allow students to use a particular color that is beneficial. The overlays can help many children process words and numbers more accurately. Use colored writing paper for students helped by this strategy.[1]
- If a student has visual problems, try the Fernald Reading Method. Using a crayon, write a word the child needs on a 5" x 8" card. Have the child trace over the word a few times with the index finger of his or her writing hand while saying the word. Then the youngster writes the word into a story.
- For youngsters with reversal problems, experiment with enlarged, simple print. In math, make numbers large and place few examples on a page.
- Provide students with their own copy of needed information if they have difficulty copying from the board.
- Deemphasize phonics for students with auditory problems.
- Try the following with youngsters experiencing memory problems: the Carbo Recorded-Book® Method (provides repetition of words within a high-interest story) and *Sight Words That Stick*™ (teaches words with cartoon-like pictures and stories).[2]
- Draw simple pictures to convey directions for students who cannot read well.
- For youngsters with handwriting difficulties, provide paper with larger spaces between lines, have them dictate their stories, and/or encourage them to use a computer or typewriter.
- Encourage teachers to share new floor games, manipulatives, etc., at faculty meetings. Set aside time on the weekly agenda.

ACCOMMODATING STUDENTS WITH AD/HD

The child with AD/HD (Attention Deficit Hyperactive Disorder) uses motion to bring his or her central nervous system to a normal state of arousal or alertness. Most students have little or no difficulty staying alert when they are still, but this is not true for the AD/HD child. These youngsters must move to stay alert—squirming, doodling, wiggling, and even chewing on clothing. AD/HD children are easily spotted in a classroom because their hands are often in constant motion, tearing paper, tapping pencils, and touching everything around them. Interestingly, they often are unaware of their own constant motion.[3]

Understandably, AD/HD children find it difficult to attend to classroom instruction or stay on task. Too much information places them in a state of overload, causing them to withdraw or "tune out." They also tend to have weak organizational skills. Their lockers and desks may be extremely messy, and they may lose their homework and forget to do assignments.

"The child with AD/HD (Attention-Deficit Hyperactive Disorder) uses motion to bring his or her central nervous system to a normal state of arousal or alertness."

What kind of instruction is needed by AD/HD children? Let's look at the AD/HD child in terms of his or her reading style strengths. AD/HD children have an exaggerated reading style. They are *extremely* tactile and kinesthetic. To function well in school, they need extremely high-interest reading materials, sufficient modeling (Chapters 4 and 5), a great deal of academically focused movement as they learn,[4] brief assignments, assistance as needed during small-group and independent work, and some calming experiences during the school day, such as soft light and music, snacks, and soft furniture.

AD/HD is a medical condition that can be difficult to diagnose. Some AD/HD children are bright and some are not. Most are boys.

Although the American Psychological Association has developed detailed criteria for identifying AD/HD youngsters, children with emotional difficulties can sometimes exhibit similar symptoms, as can highly tactile/kinesthetic youngsters who are not AD/HD.

The entire reading styles philosophy works for AD/HD students because it meets their sensory needs naturally. For purposes of instructional planning, regardless of whether the term AD/HD is used, youngsters who need to move in order to learn should have motion designed into their instruction. They need to walk, touch, and play while they learn during as much of the school day as possible.

Recommendations for Principals

- Help your teachers to understand and accommodate the reading style of the tactile, kinesthetic, global child. In an exaggerated form, this tends to be the typical reading style pattern of the AD/HD youngster.
- Above all, remember that AD/HD students require a multisensory approach to learning.
- Validate and encourage focused movement in classrooms. Have teachers create lists of strategies that allow students to experience and apply knowledge through movement.
- Encourage teachers to design a variety of instructional areas within their classrooms that allow children to move, such as informal reading areas, floor work, board work, and small-group work.
- Allow and encourage low light, snacks, and music in classrooms. These can help to calm and relax AD/HD youngsters.
- Work with your art and physical education teachers to create classroom projects that involve children's large and small muscles as they learn.
- Explore the use of a T-stool or therapy ball in place of a chair. These devices provide the constant movement many AD/HD children need. If in doubt, consult an occupational therapist.

Kinesthetic children retain information more easily when they move as they learn.

Photo courtesy of Howard Elementary School, Medford, Oregon.

A rocking motion helps this kinesthetic little girl read easily and retain the information.

Photo courtesy of Silk Hope Elementary School, Chatham County, North Carolina.

A greatly enlarged computer keyboard enables these kinesthetic youngsters to master the North Carolina standard of computer literacy.

Recommendations for Teachers

- Use a large variety of activities that accommodate the tactile/kinesthetic student, such as games, manipulatives, drama, and artwork.
- Accumulate files of effective manipulative materials and ideas. Share them with parents and staff.
- Teach with centers. If you have not employed this strategy, begin with one center that contains directions, objectives, and a variety of ways to learn and demonstrate mastery of information. You might include any or all of these elements: games, recordings, arts and crafts, worksheets.
- Tactile input stimulates the nervous system of the AD/HD child and usually improves concentration. Have "fidgets" available for youngsters who need them, such as squeeze balls, mini-puzzles, or rubber animals.

Photo courtesy of Silk Hope Elementary School, Chatham, North Carolina.

The use of a therapy ball instead of a chair provides the constant movement this AD/HD youngster needs to perform his best. When his classmates line up, he just moves the ball under his desk and lines up with them!

- Try alternative seating that allows the AD/HD child increased movement, such as therapy balls, T-stools, or, if the condition is not severe, soft furniture that allows the youngster to shift position easily.
- Provide brief assignments that are somewhat challenging but not frustrating. Check the youngster's work often and praise as appropriate.
- Provide help in organization by color-coding subjects, verifying that homework is written down and completed, giving clear directions, and scheduling quiet times for checking work.
- Try allowing students to work in pairs and in small groups to help keep the AD/HD child on task.

Tracing, feeling, and touching can speed the learning process while a patient volunteer provides warmth, encouragement, and feedback.

Photo courtesy of Anthon Elementary School, Uvalde, Texas.

Tracing letters in a sand tray enables this youngster to recognize and remember them. Notice the well-organized setting, including a plastic sheet for sitting, book displays, and a pocket chart.

Photo courtesy of Silk Hope Elementary School, Chatham County, North Carolina.

A volunteer listens to a child read and provides encouragement.

- Provide experiences that help to calm the AD/HD child, such as soft light, music, snacks, and soft furniture. Several research studies have recommended Baroque music.
- Try raps or songs containing words or information you want students to remember.
- Try turning notebook paper to the side so that the writing lines are vertical. Have students use these columns when doing computation to help keep the numbers lined up.
- Use paper with raised lines for students who have difficulty staying on the line as they write.

ACCOMMODATING GIFTED STUDENTS

Gifted children are often underserved and misunderstood in our schools. Budget cutbacks have limited services in many locales to pull-out programs for the academically and creatively gifted. Initially, gifted youngsters were identified based on I.Q. scores alone; now, however, rating scales and test scores are used in addition to or in place of the single I.Q. score.

Many states are moving quickly to serve gifted students in regular classrooms. At times, gifted youngsters are being pulled out for specific projects or areas of study. The resource room concept is being used less and less, and classroom teachers are expected to accommodate gifted youngsters through curriculum compacting, projects, and a more individualized approach to teaching. The teacher of gifted students is becoming a resource to classroom teachers, helping them to locate materials and design areas of study. Classroom teachers are also encouraged to identify those students not classified as gifted who exhibit gifted behaviors, and to include those children in projects or areas of interest.

Sometimes gifted children have difficulty learning to read. More often, they read well but may become bored and unmotivated by a school's reading program. An understanding of the reading styles of gifted youngsters is critically important.

Gifted children may have many different reading styles. When administered the Reading Style Inventory®, gifted youngsters often, but not always, score highly across all perceptual areas. Many of these children do not prefer lectures because the pace of most lectures in the regular classroom moves too slowly. They do enjoy lectures that challenge their minds; they may also enjoy self-paced activities such as teaching games, challenging software, projects, independent study, and peer teaching.

Not all gifted students are teacher-pleasers, nor do they necessarily complete paper-and-pencil work in a timely manner. They often like choices that include their own suggestions. The Individualized Reading Method tends to accommodate the reading styles of many gifted youngsters (see Glossary for description).

Recommendations for Principals

- Provide training for classroom teachers on strategies that accommodate the above-level reader.
- Meet with your faculty to discuss ways of identifying both the underachieving and culturally diverse gifted students.
- Provide financial assistance in stocking classroom libraries with reading materials that are well above grade level across a wide variety of subjects.
- Encourage teachers to place greater importance on stimulating high-level thinking skills and knowledge, rather than on neatness and punctuality alone.
- If your school employs a pull-out program for gifted students, support and enforce a policy that does not require gifted children to make up the work missed when they are not in their regular classroom.

Recommendations for Teachers

- Be flexible. Your gifted students may not need to be in the regular, on-grade-level reading program. Experiment with allowing gifted readers to read books of their choice.
- Remember that high-performing readers may still have difficulty with certain reading skills. If a youngster reads well without these skills or is unable to master them, do not teach the skills.
- Give many choices for both book selection and book projects.

> Not all gifted students are teacher-
> pleasers, nor do they necessarily complete
> paper-and-pencil work in a timely manner.

- Although gifted students often need the socialization provided by cooperative reading groups, plan times when gifted youngsters can choose to work alone.
- Remember that the gifted student is not an assistant teacher. Some enjoy assisting other students; some don't. Provide opportunities for them to work with other bright students or to work alone.
- Don't compare the work of less-capable students to the work of the gifted child. Such comparisons can be a source of embarrassment to both.
- Try curriculum compacting for students who quickly grasp new material.
- Initiate a research project.
- Encourage use of technology to expand a subject area.
- Allow students to find information using the Internet.

ACCOMMODATING BILINGUAL/LEP STUDENTS

Bilingual/LEP (Limited English Proficient) students can find it very difficult both intellectually and emotionally to learn a new language. These youngsters come to school with varying degrees of proficiency both in their native language and in English. Some bilingual youngsters are proficient in both, some in one language, and some in neither language. Those who are limited in English often feel shy and embarrassed in American classrooms.

Schools need to provide risk-free, comfortable, relaxing environments where language and academic abilities can develop naturally.[6] Possible environmental accommodations are soft music, snacks, soft light, comfortable furniture, and learning centers.

The first key to accelerate learning is knowing and understanding the bilingual youngster's reading style. The style of the

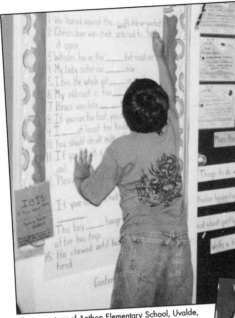

Moving, touching, writing, and feeling help these tactile and kinesthetic youngsters learn quickly.

Photo courtesy of Anthon Elementary School, Uvalde, Texas.

Filling in an oversized completion exercise provides the physical movement needed to stimulate this youngster's thinking. Answers written on the laminated chart are easily erased.

Photo courtesy of Stemley Road Elementary School, Talladega, Alabama.

Standing at a bookshelf to reproduce spelling words with letter tiles helps this kinesthetic youngster do her best.

bilingual/LEP student may vary greatly, depending on the individual and the cultural impact of his or her heritage. These youngsters learn more easily if the material is highly meaningful to them. Activities that expand upon and activate a youngster's prior knowledge are also likely to accelerate learning.

Two reading methods that have worked extremely well with bilingual youngsters are the Language-Experience Method and the Carbo Recorded-Book® Method. Both are global reading approaches that enable youngsters to develop language and reading abilities with high-interest, confidence-building activities.

The instructional recommendations that follow can be used with both ESL programs (English only) and bilingual programs (English and native language used). The strategies recommended— recording books, active learning, story writing, and so on—have been highly effective with bilingual/LEP youngsters regardless of the type of program in which they participate.

"Bilingual students need risk-free, comfortable, relaxing environments where language and academic abilities can develop naturally."

Recommendations for Principals

- Learn expressions in the native language(s) of your students. Use the expressions to help them feel accepted.
- Hold schoolwide fairs and other special events that highlight and share native foods and language, and information about culture-specific events.
- Provide teacher training on effective strategies for the bilingual student.
- Provide teachers with necessary materials and equipment, particularly manipulatives, recorded books, blank tape cassettes, listening centers, headsets, tape players, and card readers.
- Purchase books—some in English and some in the native language(s) of the students—for the school library.

- Develop and share a bank of hands-on materials and recorded books that can be used to develop English proficiency and reading skills. Develop some of these resources in the students' native language(s) as well.
- Display lots of children's writing. Encourage the development of books written by children. Laminate them, record them, and store them in the school library for student use.
- Record texts and other reading material. Duplicate these for classroom use.
- Allow students to take home and use taped books.
- Hold parent trainings on reading styles and the Continuum of Modeling Reading Methods (see Chapter 4), especially the Carbo Recorded-Book® Method.

Recommendations for Teachers

- Provide print-rich environments in English and, when feasible, in the students' native language(s).
- Validate children's native language(s) by sharing native foods, expressions, and information about culture-specific events.
- Use many small-group, interactive strategies, such as cooperative and collaborative learning.
- Stock your class library with books in English and in the native language(s) of your students.
- Use many hands-on activities, projects, and product creations.
- Use a meaning-centered curriculum to aid learning and language development.
- Gear instruction at or slightly above the students' level of language proficiency.
- Try the Language-Experience Method to teach reading and writing. This approach allows students to dictate or write interesting, simple stories and then choral-read or pair-read them for additional practice.
- Record books, magazine articles, and short stories using the Carbo Recorded-Book® Method. This method enables students to hear and see the structure of the language they are learning. Both vocabulary and understanding build quickly due to the slow pace, the small amounts of written material recorded on a tape

side, and the repetition allowed.

- When necessary, record the introduction to a story in the youngster's native language. Then record the story in English.
- Allocate ample time for students to listen to taped passages while they follow along with their finger in the text. Make certain to provide time for youngsters to read back to more proficient readers (teacher, volunteers, peers).
- Record textbooks at a regular pace and make them available for students.
- Duplicate tapes and allow students to take them home with the reading material for extra practice.

ACCOMMODATING BEHAVIORALLY/ EMOTIONALLY CHALLENGED STUDENTS

Emotionally challenged students are often targeted for special services when their behavioral patterns make learning difficult for themselves and for their classmates. Identification of the emotionally challenged student for special services should be done after specially designed educational support services and intervention strategies have been tried in the regular classroom and a youngster still exhibits patterns of inappropriate behavior.

Such behavior may make adequate academic progress impossible even though the youngster is not learning disabled. Under normal conditions, the child might exhibit inappropriate or immature types of behavior or feelings. The child may suffer from pervasive unhappiness or depression, or may have a tendency to develop physical symptoms, such as severe pains or fears associated with personal or school problems.

Whatever their origin, students' emotional difficulties can interfere strongly with learning. The needs of these students can be quite complex. The move toward inclusion may mean that these youngsters receive their academic instruction in a regular classroom with supportive services provided, or in an alternate setting.

Since the challenging condition varies from child to child, there is no dominant perceptual strength. Emotionally challenged youngsters can display a wide range of cognitive abilities. Accommodating the interests and strengths of these youngsters provides the foundation for success. A great many activities taught in the reading styles approach target their needs. Generally, emotionally challenged children profit from instructional methodology that reduces frustration and stress.

Recommendations for Principals

- Become familiar with the contract or plan for meeting the emotional and academic needs of challenged youngsters. Accept (and encourage teachers to accept) diverse types of acceptable behaviors.
- Encourage and reward classroom activities that provide the student with acceptable choices, and allow for tactile involvement and movement.
- Provide some quiet time when children can come to your office for a positive reason, such as sharing a book or project, rather than for misbehaving.
- Focus on the positive. Schedule times for teachers to share strategies that have worked with a student.
- Develop a bank of recorded books using the Carbo Recorded-Book® Method. This method offers an escape from classroom distractions while enhancing the child's reading ability.
- Develop a bank of hands-on materials that teach academic skills and can be used alone or in small groups. For some students, the interest generated by these materials can reduce unacceptable behaviors.
- Reduce the causes of disruptive behavior. Find and support activities that provide positive reinforcement on the academic level of the student.
- Encourage teachers to chart positive behavior.
- Support the classroom teacher. Establish plans for assistance if needed to manage disruptive behavior.

Recommendations for Teachers

- Create a team-developed individual educational plan (IEP). In addition to key staff members and parents or guardians, try to include the input of others who have a good relationship with the child (the custodian, the cook, a friend, etc.).

- Develop a variety of hands-on materials, such as self-checking task cards, flip chutes, and electroboards. These devices can be individualized while allowing the child some control.
- Graphically chart the child's positive behaviors. These charts should be private so that each child competes only with himself or herself.
- Develop activities that provide the student with acceptable choices. For example, the child may choose the order in which to complete tasks, or may be given a choice of two out of three tasks to complete.
- Use the Carbo Recorded-Book® Method with students who need to improve their reading. In addition to focusing the child and increasing reading fluency, the readback provides one-on-one time with the teacher.
- Challenge but try not to frustrate the children. Use self-checking materials, games, and brief assignments.
- Reduce feelings of failure and low self-worth. When grading papers, try placing checkmarks on all the correct answers. Allow the child a chance to correct those that are wrong, or work with him or her to correct them.

In Conclusion

Each youngster brings unique strengths and experiences to school that deserve to be recognized and nurtured. Business as usual in American schools—textbook-dominated instruction, short-answer evaluations, and lecture-dominated teaching—seldom works for our special needs children.

As the instructional leader, the principal must provide teachers with experiences that verify that all children can learn. Teachers need a wide variety of strategies; they need to identify and accommodate their students' strengths and needs; and they require adequate staff development, modeling, and coaching so that they are confident in using the most effective strategies for particular students.

This chapter has provided many specific recommendations for helping special needs children. For more information on successful model programs, reading styles training, and the Reading Style Inventory®, see Appendices B and D.

REFERENCES

1. H. Irlen, *Reading by the Colors: Overcoming Dyslexia and Other Reading Disabilities Through the Irlen Method* (Garden City Park, N.Y.: Avery Publishing Group, Inc., 1991).

2. M. Carbo, *How to Record Books for Maximum Reading Gains* (Syosset, N.Y.: National Reading Styles Institute, 1989; and J. Martin, *Sight Words That Stick* (Syosset, N.Y.: National Reading Styles Institute, 1996).

3. R. Barkley, *Attention Deficit Hyperactivity Disorder* (New York: Guilford Press, 1990); G. L. Flick, *Power Parenting for Children with ADD/ADHD: A Practical Parents' Guide for Managing Difficult Behaviors* (Nyack, N.Y.: Center for Applied Research in Education, 1996); C. Hannaford, *Smart Moves —Why Learning Is Not All in Your Head* (Arlington, Va.: Great Ocean Publishers, 1995); S. F. Rief, *How to Reach and Teach ADD/ADHD Children* (West Nyack, N.Y.: Center for Applied Research in Education, 1993); and K. Cummins Wunderlich, *The Teacher's Guide to Behavioral Interventions: Intervention Strategies for Behavior Problems in the Educational Environment* (Columbia, Mo.: Hawthorne Educational Services, 1988).

4. A. Green Gilbert, *Teaching the Three Rs Through Movement Experiences* (Englewood Cliffs, N.J.: Prentice-Hall, 1977); P. Kaye, *Games for Reading* (New York: Pantheon Books, 1984); P. Kaye, *Games for Learning* (New York: Noonday Press, 1991); and P. Kaye, *Games for Writing* (New York: Noonday Press, 1995); R. Thomasson, *Patterns for Hands-On Learning* (Syosset, N.Y.: National Reading Styles Institute, 1993).

5. D. Ford, *Reversing Underachievement Among Gifted Black Students* (New York: Teachers College Press, 1996); J. S. Renzulli, *Schools for Talent Development* (Mansfield Center, Conn.: Creative Learning Press, 1994); S. Yahnke Walker, *The Survival Guide for Parents of Gifted Kids* (Minneapolis: Free Spirit Publishing Co., 1994); and S. Winebrenner, *Teaching Gifted Kids in the Regular Classroom* (Minneapolis: Free Spirit Publishing Co., 1992).

6. P. Gibbons, *Learning to Learn in a Second Language* (Newtown, Australia: Heinemann, 1991); S.D. Krashen, *Bilingual Education: A Focus on Current Research,* Occasional Papers in Bilingual Education, No. 3 (Washington, D.C.: National Clearinghouse for Bilingual Education, 1991); and K. Spangenberg-Urbschat and R. Pritchard, *Kids Come in All Languages: Reading Instruction for ESL Students* (Newark, Del.: International Reading Association, 1994).

CHAPTER 8

Improving Reading Test Scores

BY MARIE CARBO AND REBECCA THOMASSON

We want our children to read well, to enjoy reading, and to read a lot. We also want them to test well. We use test results in reading to assess student achievement and teacher effectiveness, to evaluate programs and schools, and to group and place students. With reading ranked as the top educational priority in many states, children need to learn how to perform their very best on reading tests.

How can teachers and principals make the time spent preparing children to take reading tests an enjoyable and worthwhile educational experience? Often, test preparation steals time from the reading instruction and practice that students must have to become good readers. Therefore, test

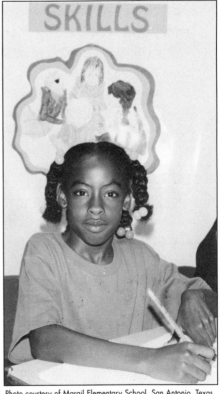

Photo courtesy of Margil Elementary School, San Antonio, Texas.

preparation should be brief. It should be fun. And it should help to improve reading skills and work habits. In other words, *test preparation should be educationally sound.*

In this chapter we discuss how to:

1. Increase voluntary reading
2. Use alternative assessments
3. Capitalize on reading styles
4. Identify test objectives
5. Practice sample items
6. Teach test-taking strategies

Photo courtesy of Roosevelt Elementary School, Medford, Oregon.

These fifth-graders take some time to read with and to their stuffed animals. Providing special times like these helps to increase voluntary reading.

Increase Voluntary Reading

First, it's clear that children need to spend most of their reading time listening to, reading, enjoying, discussing, and sharing books—*not* preparing for reading tests. The more time youngsters spend reading *because they want to,* the better they perform on reading tests. Most important, voluntary reading improves reading abilities.

There's a strong message here for educators. Throughout the school year, students need to read and discuss books. Struggling readers need to spend plenty of time hearing good reading modeled and practicing their reading (see Chapters 4-6).[1] The more comfortable students become with the sound and feel of written language, the more likely they are to perform well on reading tests.

"The more time youngsters spend reading because they want to, the better they perform on reading tests."

Spend only a small amount of time with worksheets that resemble the test. When worksheets are overused, students can become stressed and bored, and even grow to dislike reading. Using too many worksheets actually *discourages* voluntary reading. Studies released by the National Assessment of Educational Progress (NAEP) recommend a sharp *decrease* in the use of worksheets to teach reading to prepare for tests.[2]

Capitalize on Reading Styles

Everyone has a learning style for reading, or "reading style." When we accommodate students' reading style strengths, they learn more easily and perform better on tests. Children need to feel relaxed, confident, and energized while preparing for or taking tests. But if their reading styles are severely mismatched, they may feel tense or even physically ill. Anxiety, frustration, and stress sap a child's ability to learn to read or to test well.

Try incorporating the following strategies throughout the year. They should be used to prepare children to take tests, and during the actual testing period, if possible. We've found that the first two strategies are critically important for raising children's reading skills; the fourth and fifth strategies can help to relax youngsters and increase their energy.

Reading Styles Strategies to Improve Test Scores

- **Record passages.** The use of recorded books has caused high reading gains. Pre-record a story or passage to be practiced, so that low-level readers can listen to the material and follow along in the text as many times as needed. This strategy can improve fluency, comprehension, and vocabulary. As reading skills improve, the tapes can be used less and less.

- **Determine if modifications can be used.** Check with the district's testing coordinator or the state department of education's testing department. Often modifications can be used during the actual test time if they have been used throughout the school year.

- **Try colored overlays.** For some students with visual problems, letters may appear to double, swirl, or shake. Place different colored overlays over a page of print, such as a worksheet or test booklet. If one of the overlay colors makes the words appear clearer or more stable, encourage the student to continue using it.

- **Allow children healthy snacks.** Raisins, carrots, and celery sticks are appropriate. Snacking can reduce stress and increase energy. Set definite rules, and rehearse procedures before testing dates.

- **Provide comfortable seating and movement.** When children sit for long periods on hard chairs, many feel confined and uncomfortable and find it hard to concentrate. Those who need mobility should be seated in the back of the room and allowed to quietly stand and stretch at designated intervals.

Improving Test Performance

Standardized Tests—A Hard Reality. Schools are often evaluated according to their students' test scores. But do tests always reflect the actual reading ability of students? Probably not. First, paper-and-pencil tests cannot measure the dynamics of the reading process, and, second, today's tests are very often contaminated by the large amounts of practice schools give to materials that resemble the test.

Since the evaluation of many schools is based on students' test performance, let's look at some strategies that can help children to perform at their best, *without* taking an inordinate amount of time. These strategies are: identify reading objectives, teach through areas of comprehension, determine which objectives to teach, practice sample items, teach with hands-on materials, and teach test-taking skills.

Six Strategies for Improving Test Performance

1. Identify Reading Objectives. Your first step is to find out which objectives are being tested. This isn't difficult, but it may take some digging on your part. Begin by looking at booklets that list the testing objectives. Your district's central office may have this information. If not, this information is available from state education departments or from the testing companies that publish the tests.

Quite often, the major objectives tested in reading are word meaning, supporting ideas, summarization, relationships and outcomes, inferences and generalizations, point of view, propaganda, and fact versus nonfact. (Note: Phonic ability is not always measured, but can be taught if appropriate for the student's reading style.)

After learning which reading objectives are being tested, find out which of the objectives are being emphasized. While some objectives may be tested with only two items, for example, others may be tested with 20. It's likely that you'll want your teachers to put their teaching efforts into those test objectives that represent the bulk of the test items.

Here's how to determine how many test items are used to measure a test objective. Look at one student's test results by using the youngster's individual student report. Test results are reported in fractions, and the *denominator* reveals how many test items there are in a category. For example, if a student scores 3/20 in summarization, you know immediately that there are 20 items measuring summarization and the student got only three correct. If a student scores 1/2 on propaganda, there are only two items that measure propaganda and the student got one correct. *So where would you place your teaching emphasis: on summarization (20 items on the test) or on propaganda (2 items on the test)?* Definitely have your teachers take more time to teach and practice summarization if you want to raise your test scores. Exception to the rule: Suppose your students were absolute experts on summarization (they nearly top the test every time in this area!) but need work on propaganda. In this unusual case, teachers might spend more time on propaganda than they do on summarization.

2. Teach Three Areas of Comprehension. Generally, there are three different kinds of comprehension questions: recreational, textual, and functional. *Recreational* questions resemble traditional comprehension questions that usually follow a reading passage. *Textual* questions follow science and social studies reading passages; they tend to be more difficult and contain vocabulary specific to these subjects. Students must predict outcomes and draw conclusions from informational passages. The third area of comprehension is *functional*, which surprises many educators. Here students are asked to interpret charts and graphs, and to follow directions.

3. Determine Which Objectives to Teach. Analyze prior test results to determine students' weakest areas. (You might use the class summary from the group's previous test.) Study the results of the lowest two or three objectives. Were these objectives taught? If so, did the students understand what was taught? Should the objectives be retaught using a methodology that matches students' perceptual strengths?

Teachers can also look at the test results of the lowest-scoring students, and then teach the objectives that received the lowest overall scores. These should be taught through the student's

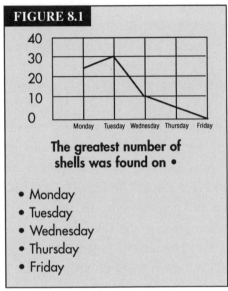

FIGURE 8.1

The greatest number of shells was found on •

- Monday
- Tuesday
- Wednesday
- Thursday
- Friday

Many functional questions involve interpreting graphs and charts. This electroboard sheet provides practice that is fun and allows movement. See Figure 8.4 for instructions.

strengths, which in most cases will be tactile (hands-on) and kinesthetic (body in motion).

In teaching the unmastered objectives, teachers can help students by using the language of the test. For example, in working on sequencing, use test language such as *prior, between*, and *after* instead of *first, second*, and *third*.

4. Practice Sample Items. Many teachers require students to practice worksheets that closely resemble the actual test. This type of practice does help children to become familiar with a particular test format, but it has little effect on students' performance on other types of tests. It can be used for very brief periods a few weeks before the test.[3] In the remainder of this chapter, we'll discuss some techniques that can improve students' test-taking skills and work habits.

5. Teach with Hands-On Materials. Hands-on materials are a child-friendly way to teach test objectives.[4] Most elementary-age children, especially low achievers, are strongly tactile. Tactile students benefit greatly from practicing a specific skill with tactile resources, such as games (Figures 8.1, 8.2, and 8.3). After the students master the skill with these resources,

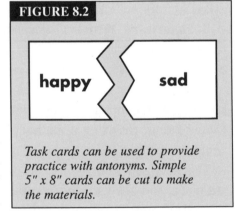

FIGURE 8.2

happy   sad

Task cards can be used to provide practice with antonyms. Simple 5" x 8" cards can be cut to make the materials.

they can work on that skill in the more difficult format of a worksheet or test booklet.

It's important to replicate the test format when designing hands-on materials. Often the students know the materials, but they may need some time to adjust to the format. Sample test booklets can be used with an item-matching device called an electroboard (see Figure 8.4).

Try response cards. Simple response cards can be a very effective way of involving children tactilely and kinesthetically. This activity allows teachers to see quickly which students are mastering each objective. Suppose, for example, that students are learning how to distinguish between fact and opinion. Each child might be given two response cards, with one of two letters printed on each card: F (fact)

Multiple meanings of words (vocabulary section) are practiced with this electroboard example.

FIGURE 8.4

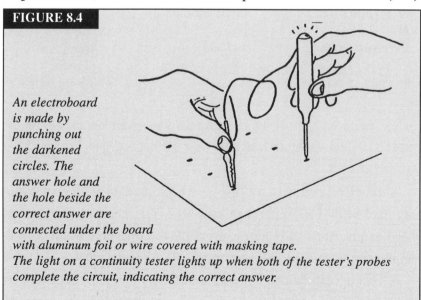

An electroboard is made by punching out the darkened circles. The answer hole and the hole beside the correct answer are connected under the board with aluminum foil or wire covered with masking tape. The light on a continuity tester lights up when both of the tester's probes complete the circuit, indicating the correct answer.

Using Bloom's Taxonomy to Improve Test Scores

To improve scores on tests that involve high-level thinking skills, direct a major portion of class activities to Evaluation, Synthesis, and Analysis.

Requires Highest Thinking Skills

Evaluation
Argue   Judge   Predict   Validate

Synthesis
Design   Develop   Expand   Modify

Analysis
Analyze   Defend   Compare   Classify

Application
Illustrate   Demonstrate   Indicate   Record

Understanding
Explain   Rephrase   Conclude   Justify

Knowledge
List   Label   Identify   State

Requires Lowest Thinking Skills

or O (opinion). The teacher makes a statement about a story or passage. Then each student holds up the appropriate card with the correct answer.

Another related activity provides each student with four cards, one each with A, B, C, or D printed on it. The teacher uses the overhead or a worksheet to present a sample test question. Students hold up the response card with the correct item choice.

6. Teach Test-Taking Strategies. Many youngsters need to learn *how* to take tests. Here is one of our favorite strategies for developing comprehension skills. Since many low-performing students have global tendencies and prefer to work in small groups or pairs, every week or so assign students in pairs to read a sample comprehension test item. (A global approach would be to read the questions first, and then search the passage for the answer.)

- *Highlight the Question and Answer with the*
  Same Color Highlighter

Using highlighting pens or markers, the students highlight the first question with, say, the green marker. Then they search the passage for the correct answer and highlight it with the same color. Together they read the possible answers and highlight their chosen answer in green.

The second question would be highlighted with a different color, and the same procedures followed. If the answer to the question isn't stated exactly, there would be no corresponding highlighted color in the passage. Since many test questions are often inferential in nature, this strategy is a visual means of "seeing" that not all test questions have definite answers.

- *Remove Highlighters Before Test Time*

To help students prepare for the length of the many comprehension questions on the test, add one, two, and then three passages to

Photo courtesy of Robb Elementary School, Uvalde, Texas.

A second-grader performs for his teacher. By making frequent notes of a student's performance, teachers can evaluate a student's abilities and needs.

be completed at one sitting. Four to six weeks before testing time, take away the highlighters if your state does not allow their use during the actual test, and request that students complete the activity alone, instead of in groups.

This approach to practicing comprehension skills is especially helpful for tactile children. It also allows students to work together in groups, to search for information in context, to use color (which appeals to the right-hemispheric person), and to discuss the answers. The student's time is spent *learning the objective* instead of randomly marking answers to the questions. It's an excellent reinforcer for remembering: each answer pops right out from the page.

Recommendations for Principals

- During a faculty meeting, lead a session on analyzing class test scores from the previous test administered. Help teachers within small groups to analyze their own class test results.
- Identify the teachers whose students scored the highest on various objectives. Ask for their suggestions regarding how they taught those objectives. Know your faculty. If personalities permit, ask the more effective teachers to share their techniques at a faculty meeting they conduct. If it is best not to feature the teacher(s), present a handout with a brief description of the strategies yourself.
- After analyzing test results, determine those objectives on which students demonstrated the lowest level of performance. Hold brainstorming sessions with the faculty on how to raise student performance on these objectives.
- Correlate the test objectives with your curriculum guides and textbooks to determine if the objectives weretaught that year.
- Have each faculty member self-evaluate to determine if he/she taught the objectives. If the objectives were taught after the testing date, then correct the order in which objectives are taught.
- Have the faculty develop methods to teach the objectives through the visual, auditory, tactile, and kinesthetic perceptual strengths.
- Take an *active* role yourself in helping teachers to reach the lowest-performing students. Remember the importance of raising the reading levels of these students in order to raise test scores.

Recommendations for Teachers

After you receive information concerning the test objectives, plan how you will emphasize the test items that are most heavily tested. The only exception to this practice is in the area of phonics. If the student is not auditory and analytic, then the student may never be able to actually "hear" phonics. To some degree, phonics is tested visually on an achievement test. Work with these children to notice visual patterns that might indicate the correct answer. A limited amount of time should be spent on this activity.

- Study the test results for your class from last year. Determine the objectives on which your students scored poorly. Determine whether or not you taught these objectives. If you did not, then include them in the current teaching year. If you did teach the objectives and the students did not learn them, then try to determine the reason and how you can remedy the situation (especially see Chapters 5 and 6 for strategies).

- Ask other teachers for strategies they use to teach objectives that are not mastered well by your students.

- Try recording sample test passages. As your students work with these recordings, they will become familiar with the test language and the levels of the material to be read.

- Study last year's test results of your current class. Identify two or three students with the lowest scores. Teach those objectives through the students' perceptual strengths.

- Remember that low-performing students are often tactile/kinesthetic youngsters. Teach test objectives through recordings, games, and kinesthetic activities (see Chapters 5 and 6). After your objectives are mastered by the youngsters using a game format, then transfer the material to the paper-and-pencil format. As testing dates grow nearer (within one month or so), increase the use of pencil-and-paper activities that practice test objectives.

Best Preparation Is Reading

The best preparation for learning to be a lifelong reader is reading. Lots and lots of reading. And lots of reading is also a student's best preparation for test taking. When test preparation actually helps to improve students' reading skills and work habits, you know you're helping that youngster become a life-long reader.

Chapter 9 will discuss how to evaluate your reading program all year long to assure that it both nurtures a love of reading and helps students to test well.

REFERENCES

1. M. Carbo, "What Reading Achievement Tests Should Measure to Increase Literacy in the U.S," *Research Bulletin*, No. 7 (Bloomington, Ind.: Phi Delta Kappa, Center on Evaluation, Development, and Research, 1988).

2. *1994 NAEP Reading: A First Look, Findings from the National Assessment of Educational Progress* (Washington, D.C.: U.S. Education Department, Office of Educational Research and Improvement, 1994).

3. J. Prell and P.A. Prell, "Improving Test Scores – Teaching Test Wiseness: A Review of the Literature," *Research Bulletin*, No. 5 (Bloomington, Ind.: Phi Delta Kappa, Center on Evaluation, Development, and Research, 1986).

4. R. Thomasson, *Patterns for Hands-On Learning* (Syosset, N.Y.: National Reading Styles Institute, 1993).

Evaluating Reading Programs

How Effective Is Your Reading Program?

This chapter explores evaluation strategies that can improve the effectiveness of your reading program throughout the school year and increase the likelihood that your students will read well, love to read, and perform well on reading tests.

First we'll look at a model textbook adoption process that can be used to evaluate reading materials. Next let's explore ways to evaluate the effectiveness of your current reading program.

A Model Textbook Evaluation Process

This evaluation process, developed by Dave Adams and Cicely Cerqui, assesses five major areas: quality of the reading material, comprehension, vocabulary, decoding, and the reading/writing connection.[1] By using the checklists that accompany each section, teams of teachers, parents, and students can evaluate any reading text before adoption.

Quality of the Reading Material

In general, high-quality literature is writing by real authors that may include fictional, non-fictional, biographical, or expository works from various cultures. Children can become highly motivated by top-quality literature and will learn how to read quickly if the correct modeling methods are also used (Chapter 4).

☐ The writing can be read aloud by an adult in an interesting, natural manner.

☐ The language is meaningful, natural, and predictable.

☐ The stories appeal greatly to children.

☐ The writing provides children with insights into behavior, ethical issues, and values.

☐ The work has special qualities that appeal to children, such as humor, pattern, color, and high-quality illustrations.

☐ Text and illustrations work well together.

Comprehension

Effective instruction to assist comprehension provides a variety of strategies that enable teachers to effectively teach students to understand and apply comprehension skills to text. Comprehension questions should assist teachers in preparing students to read the text and assessing students' level of understanding of the reading material.

Comprehension Checklist

☐ Comprehension questions relate directly to the story.

☐ Three levels of comprehension questions are included: literal, interpretive, and applied.

☐ Emphasis is placed on interpretive and applied-level questions, such as What do you think...? How would you feel...? What would you do if...?

☐ Skills are clearly defined and taught.

☐ Skills are sometimes taught prior to reading to help students understand a story.

☐ Follow-up activities effectively reinforce skills.

☐ A reteaching strand provides new and different approaches for reviewing the material.

☐ Coverage of important skills is sufficient.

Vocabulary Development

Effective vocabulary instruction uses students' prior knowledge to enhance comprehension and expands the meaning of words beyond the text through the use of effective instructional strategies.

Vocabulary Checklist

☐ Specific vocabulary words have been identified from each story.

☐ Words are grouped for instruction based on their importance to the story and their level of difficulty. They receive different instructional emphasis.

☐ Vocabulary activities are varied and motivating.

☐ Children's prior knowledge and experiences are incorporated into instruction.

☐ Throughout the text, vocabulary is enhanced and expanded with mapping, categorization, and hands-on activities.

☐ Follow-up activities effectively reinforce vocabulary development through a variety of strategies and techniques.

Decoding

A high-quality decoding program teaches students skills and strategies that can be independently applied to text. A first-rate decoding program includes a variety of strategies.

Decoding Checklist

☐ A systematic phonics program is taught using meaningful context.

☐ Phonics lessons are brief and do not dominate the instruction.

☐ The phonics skills taught are important and useful.

☐ Context clues are taught.

☐ Structural-analysis skills are taught.

☐ A logical, sequential approach is used.

☐ Appropriate practice activities are included.

☐ Skills interface with stories effectively.

☐ Not every child is expected to learn each skill and strategy presented. Students' individual reading styles are recognized. Children are taught to use the strategies that match their strengths.

Reading/Writing Connection

There is strong evidence that when students respond to reading through writing they become more competent in both skills.

Reading/Writing Checklist

☐ There are clear opportunities for students to be actively involved in writing activities.

☐ A wide variety of strategies are used to stimulate, enrich, and guide children's writing.

☐ Graphic organizers assist students in their writing.

☐ A reasonable amount of invented spelling is allowed in the early grades.

☐ Correct spellings of words needed for writing are provided.

☐ There is good application to content-area writing (writing of letters, essays, lists, summaries, stories).

"First and foremost, children need to feel interested, fascinated, and excited about what they're reading."

Evaluating Your Reading Program

By answering the following four key questions, principals and supervisors can become more aware of the effectiveness of their current reading program. Each question is followed by its own evaluation strategies and recommendations.[2]

KEY QUESTION #1:
Are Your Reading Materials Interesting to Students?

Your students will make faster progress in reading if they are extremely interested in what they're reading and if the reading material challenges but doesn't defeat them. Motivation increases our ability to learn and to remember what we have learned. First and foremost, children need to feel interested, fascinated, and *excited* about what they're reading. Teachers also need to feel enthusiastic about the reading material, so they can convey their enthusiasm to students.

Evaluating Students' Interest

Evaluate students' interest in their reading materials by observing their behavior (and that of their teachers) during reading.

Are they on task? Do their facial expressions, body language, and language convey extreme interest in the material?

> ## "Include children and teachers as evaluators when adopting new texts."

Next, ask a sampling of your students and teachers about the school's reading program. Do they think it's interesting, fun, exciting, boring? What do they like or dislike about it? Would they like to change the program? How?

Recommendations for Principals

• Include children and teachers as evaluators when adopting new texts.

• Evaluate the stories your students are currently reading, and eliminate those that the children don't enjoy or find boring, as well as those that the teachers dislike. Do the same with any

Photo courtesy of Carbonaro Elementary School, Valley Stream, New York.

Provide a wide variety of high-interest reading materials.

workbook pages. This process can be done by grade-level teams and will help to provide teachers with the best reading material for their students.

Recommendations for Teachers

• Interview children about their reading interests. Stock classroom libraries with reading material based on their interests.

- Encourage students to bring their favorite books to school and share them.
- Expand students' interests with books on less familiar topics. Read excerpts of these books aloud, and engage children in discussions of the material to stimulate interest.

Photo courtesy of Bob Hope Elementary School, San Antonio, Texas.

Students should be engaged in what they're reading. They should also be provided with sufficient modeling to achieve success.

KEY QUESTION #2:
Do Your Students Read Fluently?

You want your students to read with ease. Students who struggle as they decipher words are unlikely to become motivated or competent readers. Fluency enables children to concentrate on the meaning of what they're reading rather than on the process of figuring out the words.

Evaluating Reading Fluency

To find the general levels of fluency of students in your school, randomly select about 20 youngsters at different reading and grade levels and ask each privately to read a passage on his or her level. Are the children confident and happy as they read? Does their reading flow easily? Do they phrase the material well? Or is the whole experience laborious and embarrassing for them?

Next, observe the behavior of children during reading lessons in their classroom. Do they volunteer to read aloud often and enthusiastically, or do they shrink back or even act out aggressively? Finally, are many of your students reading fluently only at levels well below expectations?

Improving Reading Fluency

Improving reading fluency requires students to learn with reading methods that capitalize on their strengths, and teachers to use many methods that model good reading. The following suggestions for teachers can help to sharply increase students' reading fluency.

Recommendations for Principals

• Foster a school-wide emphasis on reading.

• Assist the parent support group in sponsoring parent/student reading times.

• Have members of your faculty present a program to the parents explaining the Continuum of Modeling Reading Methods (Chapter 4). A brief demonstration of the methods will assist parents in helping with children's reading at home.

• Arrange for the purchase of the Reading Style Inventory®, and provide training for the teachers in implementing its suggestions.

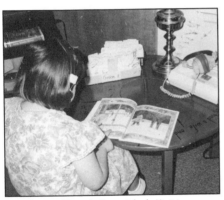

Photo courtesy of Roanoke County Schools, Virginia.

• Stock each classroom with a listening center and tape players so that children can listen to recorded materials in privacy. Make this an important budget item if reading fluency is a problem for your students.

Provide well-stocked libraries with recordings of books for students who need the modeling.

Photo courtesy of Roanoke County Schools, Virginia.

Recommendations for Teachers

- Read aloud interesting books to children often to familiarize them with written language (Chapter 1).
- Identify students' strengths with the Reading Style Inventory®, and use the recommended reading methods that capitalize on those strengths. Emphasize reading methods that capitalize on strengths (Chapters 2 and 3).
- Write stories dictated by the students on large chartpaper. Read the stories to the children at a slightly slow pace, with good expression, while pointing to the words. Repeat this process often. Have the children choral-read small parts as they are ready. As their fluency increases, have them read in pairs and, finally, alone (Chapter 4).
- Record many high-interest books with the Carbo Recorded-Book® Method described in Chapter 5. (Books are read at a slightly slower than usual pace, with special phrasing. A small amount of material is placed on each tape side, and students listen to the tape two or three times while looking at the reading material.) Teachers should work toward having 25-50 different recorded books, stories, or articles in their classroom library.
- Have students choral-read recorded passages they have heard. When fluent, youngsters can pair-read the passages or read them aloud to a teacher or volunteer.

KEY QUESTION #3: Is Good Reading Modeled Sufficiently?

If students come to school having had little experience with books (or with English), then large amounts of modeling will be necessary to enable them to overcome their lack of experience during their preschool years.

Many underachievers do not receive even minimal amounts of modeling of good reading (e.g., being read to, choral reading, or working with recorded books). When children cannot read fluently, they need to hear and see stories modeled repeatedly before being asked to read.

If the following four conditions exist in your reading program, most students will learn to read fluently and well: 1) The atmosphere is accepting and relaxed. 2) Teachers use correct reading methods consistently. 3) Sufficient modeling has occurred before children are asked to read. 4) Children have ample time to practice reading.

Evaluating the Time Students Spend Reading

You want your teachers to balance their reading program so that students spend an appropriate amount of time hearing and seeing good reading modeled, practicing their reading, and developing high-level comprehension skills. Here are questions to help guide the process.

Recommendations for Principals

• Evaluate the time students spend reading by observing children during reading lessons.
• Use the following questions to aid your observation:
  - Is a competent reader providing an excellent model of what good reading sounds like?
  - How much time do children actually spend hearing and seeing printed material as good reading is modeled during the school day?
  - Is the amount of time sufficient? (It is if the children can read back the material fluently.)

 Here's a strong danger sign: You observe that children are expected to read aloud when they are unfamiliar with a passage. They stumble over words and agonize through the material. Ask teachers how much time they spend modeling good reading for their students so that their students hear and see the words and make the connection between spoken and written language.

Recommendations for Teachers

Improving the Time Students Spend Reading

Good readers can spend a great deal of their reading time actually reading books on their own. Nonfluent readers need to spend more of their time hearing and seeing good reading modeled. Allocate about 30 to 60 minutes daily for nonfluent readers to see and hear good reading being modeled. For struggling, low-level readers, these amounts of time should be considered a minimum:

Photo courtesy of Roosevelt Elementary School, Medford, Oregon.

Good readers can spend a great deal of their time actually reading books on their own.

- 15 to 30 minutes—Have a good reader read high-interest books as the children look at the words (preferably in small groups or one-on-one), with a slightly slow pace and somewhat exaggerated expression, while pointing to the words.
- 10 to 15 minutes—Have students follow along in their books as they listen to and then read back passages that have been specially recorded.
- 5 to 15 minutes—Choral-read with the students, and use the echo method (a good reader reads a sentence or two, and the student reads back, or "echoes," the same material).

As fluency improves, less time can be spent modeling good reading, and more time can be spent allowing children to practice their reading (in pairs or alone). When children do become fluent with certain books or passages, they can read this material to less fluent readers, thus providing a good reading model for others—and boosting their own self-confidence and self-esteem.

KEY QUESTION #4: Do Your Students Comprehend at High Levels?

Now let's take the next big step. How well do your students understand what they're reading? Most current reading tests emphasize higher levels of thinking because that's the kind of thinking needed if the U.S. is going to be able to compete on a global level. High levels of thinking cannot wait for the upper grades; they must pervade instruction at *every* grade.

Students need to be able to summarize, analyze, interpret, evaluate, and predict. Those high-level thinking skills need to be learned and practiced throughout the school day, whether or not students are fluent readers. These experiences are especially important for underachievers. Research tells us that, compared to high achievers, underachievers are asked or expected to answer many fewer high-level questions.

Evaluating Reading Comprehension

Here too, begin by observing your teachers and students. What level of questions do teachers tend to ask? What kinds of questions do students answer easily? What's the percentage of low-level and high-level questions? Low-level questions ask students simply to regurgitate explicitly stated information; high-level questions require students to think about answers that are not obvious or explicitly stated in a text. You want your teachers to ask questions of each type throughout the school day. Even in the primary grades, we should be asking more high-level questions.

The following types of questions usually require only low levels of thinking: "How many children went on the trip?" "What were their names?" "Who fell in the water?" The following types of

Photo courtesy of Margil Elementary School, San Antonio, Texas.

Listening to students as they discuss their work is an excellent way to evaluate students' progress.

119

questions, on the other hand, generally require much higher levels of thinking: "Tell me the most important things the children did to keep warm" (requires summary and analysis); "Why did the accident happen?" (requires analysis and interpretation); "How could the accident have been prevented?" (requires analysis and evaluation); "What do you think will happen next? Why?" (requires analysis and prediction); and "How would you feel if that happened to you? Why?" (requires identification with the character, analysis, and validation).

Recommendations for Principals

- If necessary, provide in-service training on incorporating higher-order thinking skills into the classroom. A possible in-school facilitator might be a teacher of the gifted education class.
- Encourage the teachers to develop their lesson plans with the verbs from Bloom's Taxonomy, stressing those that provide for analysis, synthesis, and evaluation. (See Figure 8.5 for an example.)

Photo courtesy of Stemley Road Elementary School, Talladega, Alabama.

Evaluation is not an end-of-the-year event. At Stemley Road Elementary School, teachers evaluate student performance on a regular basis.

120

Recommendations for Teachers

- Improve students' understanding and vocabulary by reading to them often. Use excellent expression and books that contain many illustrations. Show and discuss the illustrations before reading.
- Constantly relate stories to children's experiences.
- Provide real experiences throughout the school day that require students to think and evaluate.
- Model high-level thinking by actually thinking aloud your own answers to high-level questions.
- Pose high-level questions to children often. Allow them to discuss and support their answers in small groups.
- Have students design and pose their own high-level questions.

"Constantly relate stories to children's experiences."

Evaluation is not an end-of-the-year event. It needs to take place throughout the school year so that reading programs constantly improve. You want your students to be *interested* in what they're reading, to be taught with the *correct reading methods* consistently, to hear *good reading modeled* sufficiently for fluency to occur, to be given *enough time* to learn to read, to be placed in experiences that require them to *think at the highest possible levels*, and to be given some *practice at taking tests*. Work toward all those conditions so that your students will become young people who read well, who love to read, and who perform well on reading tests.

REFERENCES

1. D. Adams and C. Cerqui, *A Model Textbook Adoption Process* (Seattle: Shoreline School District, 1989).

2. M. Carbo, "What Every Principal Should Know About Evaluating Reading Programs," *Instructional Leader,* vol. 8, no. 1, 1995, pp. 1-3, 12.

Learning to read should
be easy and fun.

Photo courtesy of Margil Elementary School, San Antonio, Texas.

Photo courtesy of Sacred Heart Academy, Hempstead, New York.

CHAPTER 10

How Three Principals Started Exemplary Reading Programs

BY MARIE CARBO AND REBECCA THOMASSON

How do I begin? That's the question most commonly asked by principals. In this final chapter, we'll study how three principals started and developed exemplary reading programs by using a combination of reading styles strategies and sound staff development practices.[1] Collectively, these principals work with a wide variety of students, including inner-city, rural, suburban, poor, and privileged.

Case Study #1 - Diane Crawford

When Diane Crawford became principal of Robb Elementary School six years ago, many of her fourth-graders (Robb's only grade

Photo courtesy of Robb Elementary School, Uvalde, Texas.

Principal Diane Crawford (far left) listens as a second-grader reads aloud a story his teacher has read to him several times.

at that time) had reading difficulties. Now, three years into her reading styles program, Robb's students have made impressive gains in motivation, behavior, and achievement. After just one year of the reading styles program, Uvalde assistant superintendent Barbara Skipper reported that Robb's "students' scores on the state reading test jumped from 46 percent demonstrating mastery of the subject to 73 percent demonstrating mastery."[2]

Data on Robb Elementary School

Located: Uvalde, Texas, a farming and ranching community.

Students: 540 K-4, 85% Hispanic, 15% Anglo, 85% qualify for free or reduced lunch. Pupil/teacher ratio about 20:1.

Special Notes: Many students aren't fluent in standard Spanish or standard English. About 10% participate in bilingual classes. There are units for emotionally disturbed and mentally retarded students, who are mainstreamed as much as possible.

Starting a Reading Styles Program

Diane Crawford faced three major problems in improving her reading program:

- Non-readers and poor readers generally lacked language ability.
- Each grade level was taught in a different school. Entirely different methods of teaching reading were being used with each grade level.

Photo courtesy of Robb Elementary School, Uvalde, Texas.

Some students at Robb Elementary read in comfort and others play a reading game under the chalkboard, as their teacher listens to a child read.

124

Students at Robb Elementary have fun playing a reading game. Notice the listening center and books nearby.

- In Robb's literature-based reading program, students participated in holistic activities, but weren't expected to read independently on grade level.

The Uvalde school district searched to establish a more consistent, districtwide reading program. A committee of K-12 teachers was so impressed by a reading styles presentation that the district decided to try this approach for a summer program. Using grant funds, the district organized a "mini summer school" and trained a core group of teachers. The summer program was so successful that the training was extended district-wide to all elementary teachers who taught reading.

Robb's Results

Here are the major results of Robb's three-year reading styles program, as described by Diane Crawford:

- Children read more fluently, with better comprehension and confidence.
- Students' spoken and written English has improved.
- The first-grade retention rate dropped from 8.9% to 1.7%.
- Reading scores improved substantially. After the four-week summer school program for 42 first-graders, there was a 3.5 month reading gain, with grade-equivalent scores rising from a

range of K - 2.0 to a range of 1.0 - 2.3.

- Statewide reading scores of the students who continued in the program for the next year rose from 46% to 73%.
- Voluntary reading increased. Students check out significantly more books, and participation in the Electronic Bookshelf Reading Program increased "tremendously."
- Parents are extremely supportive. They feel that the accommodation of their child's strengths is evidence of the teachers' "loving and caring about the students and going the 'extra mile'."
- Reading styles strategies extend into the home. Parents meet with teachers three times during the school year to discuss how to capitalize on their child's strengths at home.
- Behavior problems lessened even though more students now qualify as "emotionally disturbed." Frustration was reduced with tactile/kinesthetic activities that motivated the students to learn. Instead of visiting the principal for punitive measures, students went to the office to read to the principal!

Recommended First Steps

Diane recommends these six beginning steps:

- *Set weekly goals and have regular meetings to evaluate what worked and what didn't.* One week Diane's staff might focus on classroom environments, touring different rooms and then discussing what they saw and how the students responded. Networking, sharing ideas and successful techniques, and discussing students' progress helped build the strength of the program.
- *Receive the reading styles training and stay involved throughout the program.* Diane received training in reading styles right along with her staff. One day a fourth-grader and her teacher were doing cheerleader-type "alphabet cheers"—saying letters and forming them with their bodies. Understanding the importance of the activity, Diane simply observed and walked on. She learned later that something in the brain of that child had "clicked" during the cheerleading process and soon after the youngster passed spelling tests by feeling herself physically creating the letters with her body.

Photo courtesy of Robb Elementary School, Uvalde, Texas.

Two friends at Robb Elementary test each other on their reading skills using a flip chute and word cards.

- *Organize banks of materials for teachers to share.* Parent volunteers, teacher aides, and teachers can create recorded books and materials for the tactile/kinesthetic learner.

- *Keep your sense of humor.* There will be a certain amount of trial-and-error learning. Example: A group of Diane's parents got a huge supply of free milk cartons from the local Dairy Queen to make learning games for every student in the school. The tactile learners loved them, but many others didn't need or want them.

- *Encourage students to read to you.* Diane keeps a "V.I.P." book in her office, which is signed by students who go there to read to her. One boy who could not read at all went to Diane's office frequently to read aloud and show her which books his class was reading. When moving on to middle school, he told his teacher, "I'm getting a little worried. I wonder who will keep Ms. Crawford up on all the books for the class."

- *Be creative in finding needed materials.* Many of the materials needed to implement a reading styles approach can be found within the district or local community. Sometimes local businesses are happy to help.

Overall Evaluation

Diane Crawford considers the reading styles approach "one of the most cost-effective programs a school can be involved in." She and other educators saw a big difference after just two days of training, and the "wars over reading programs" disappeared.

Most of all, Diane is impressed with the difference the program has made in individual children's lives. Her students are more successful, confident, and happier. "I challenge you to find the emotionally disturbed students in our classrooms," says Diane, and she cites the case of a fourth-grader who couldn't read and instead turned over desks, threw books at other students, and stabbed himself with scissors. After the reading styles program began, he walked into the library one day and asked the librarian and Ms. Crawford to listen to him read. As Diane put it, "Even if only that one child had been helped, it was worth the journey just to see him become a functional student."

Case Study #2 - Kay Pantier

Kay Pantier became principal of R.E. Baker Elementary School in 1995, having served as assistant principal there for four years. Early in 1992, R.E. Baker was placed on a school improvement plan by the Arkansas state department of education due to below-average reading scores. By 1995, Baker had the highest Title I reading gains in the school district.

Photo courtesy of R.E. Baker Elementary School, Bentonville, Arkansas.

Words, words, words! Kay Pantier reviews vocabulary with a group of children.

Photo courtesy R.E. Baker Elementary School, Bentonville, Arkansas.

This puppet show was written, produced, and acted by one student at R.E. Baker.

Data on R.E. Baker Elementary School

Located: Bentonville, Arkansas, Wal-Mart's corporate headquarters, has corporate and rural elements with a small-town feel.

Students: 550 K-5, primarily Anglo, 45% qualify for free or reduced lunch, 5% from high-income families. Pupil/teacher ratio regulated by state law is 20:1 (kindergarten), 24:1 (grades 1-3), and 27:1 (grades 4-6).

Special Notes: Kay reports a "dramatic increase" in students diagnosed as AD/HD, those taking anti-depressant or other medication, and children "labeled" prior to starting kindergarten. R.E. Baker has a small but growing number of ESL students.

Photo courtesy R.E. Baker Elementary School, Bentonville, Arkansas.

A unit about Africa inspired this student to produce a dramatic play complete with hand puppets and scenery.

Starting a Reading Styles Program

Improving students' reading scores became a priority at R.E. Baker in 1992. The school's reading program was primarily basal-driven. After one day of reading styles inservice, teachers began implementing the reading styles strategies that correlated with Baker's reading program. By 1994 the faculty voted unanimously to focus on reading styles as a way to improve reading skills and fluency.

Funding for staff development was obtained through a Rockefeller Foundation grant, which provided $7,500 each year for five years. These funds plus local fund-raisers enabled the Baker faculty over three years to receive training on site. Kay Pantier and several of her teachers became reading styles trainers; many attended NRSI conferences. According to Kay, "staff development was definitely the key."

R.E. Baker's Results

Kay Pantier reports these results:

- After the first year, reading scores across all grade levels rose 9%, and voluntary reading and library usage increased substantially.
- From the inception of the program in 1992 until 1995, first-graders' reading scores rose from 47 NCE's (1991), to 60 NCE's (1992), to 64 NCE's (1993), to 77 NCE's (1994), to 81 NCE's (1995).
- From the fall of 1995 to the fall of 1996, the reading scores of the fourth-graders rose from 50 to 65 NCE's. Their test scores improved across subject areas. In that same time period, NCE scores rose from 45 to 51 NCE's in language, 48 to 67 NCE's in science, and 41 to 45 NCE's in social studies.
- Parents became "incredibly supportive." In 1995, 20 volunteered in Kay's building compared to 119 in 1996.
- R.E. Baker's faculty developed a central focus and common terminology that improved the staff's ability to effectively teach reading to a wide range of students. The reading styles approach was "very accommodating to diversity and special needs."

Recommended First Steps

Kay refers to these eight keys when describing how she began:

- *Obtain funding. Training is the key.* Use funds from local fund raisers, grants, or your district. Often local businesses will provide funding for reading improvement.
- *Begin with the entire staff.* Reading style strategies are everywhere at Baker. The music teacher uses games and interactive

bulletin boards; in physical education students practice vocabulary and spelling during calisthenics; art history is integrated with reading and writing projects; and the media specialist uses dance and singing to teach reading skills.

- *Identify goals to achieve.* Kay suggests that goals be stated clearly and displayed regularly in order to increase awareness and build support. Both the teachers and the students at Baker set their own personal goals.
- *Identify strengths with the Reading Style Inventory®.* The RSI is used to determine the methods, materials, and strategies that match students' strengths (see Chapter 3). Kay and her teachers have found that having access to RSI information, as well as a school-wide central focus and common terminology, has helped R.E. Baker teach a wide range of students to read well.
- *Include the custodian and cook.* Since reading styles involves the use of snacks to help children while reading, custodians may be concerned about cleanup. Make children totally responsible for cleanup after snacks, and reassure your cook that the use of snacks will not interfere with the preparation or consumption of lunch.
- *Implement throughout all grades.* At Baker, all the grades discussed their students' strengths and how each youngster learns differently. Teachers created classroom reading styles bulletin boards and talked with students about styles. A hallway bulletin board focused on the reading styles of the

Photo courtesy R.E. Baker Elementary School, Bentonville, Arkansas.

This clever device created by teachers at R.E. Baker Elementary is a belt containing word families from the week's activities.

131

teachers. (Reading styles stickers around a teacher's photograph described that teacher's style.)

- *Organize parent trainings.* Baker's staff provided reading styles information at PTA meetings and organized a "Parent University" where parents are offered choices of mini-sessions on reading styles.
- *Provide maintenance training.* Kay recommends continued trainings, demonstration lessons, and coaching for teachers even after a high level of implementation is achieved. She feels that it's extremely important to send some staff to the National Reading Styles Conference and to have an NRSI consultant conduct an on-site training once or twice yearly.

Overall Evaluation

Kay Pantier found that change is more difficult for some people than others. She recommends starting slowly and integrating reading styles with existing programs. She also strongly recommends the provision of education and training for staff members, parents, and students.

Kay points out that the change process, while never easy, is well worth the effort in the case of the reading styles program. She recalls seeing a note from a formerly low-achieving, hyperactive third-grader that said of his reading styles class:

> "I love this class! If I need to go to the informal area, I can, and the teacher never gets mad. I can learn spelling words moving and dancing, and she doesn't get mad. If I need to have a snack, it's okay. I just love this class!"

By fourth grade, the boy was reading at grade level and was doing well academically.

Case Study #3 - Doris Tidwell

Doris Tidwell has been principal of Park Hills Elementary School for 17 years. A few years ago, she and her staff became increasingly dissatisfied with their students' reading scores. After trying a number of approaches, Park Hills adopted a reading styles program. Now reading scores are up across grade levels.

This little girl has completed her book recording and has just started to read the passage aloud to principal Doris Tidwell.

Data on Park Hills Elementary School

Located: Spartanburg, North Carolina, inner-city.

Students: 500 K-6, predominantly African-American, 75% qualify for free or reduced-price lunch. Pupil/teacher ratio is 22:1.

Special Notes: About 25% of the students live in a subsidized housing project; the parents or guardians of 75% own their homes or rent single-family houses. The Title I program is school-wide, with only 8% of the students identified as needing special education or ESL services.

Starting a Reading Styles Program

Until 1992, the reading program at Park Hills was mainly basal-driven. Dissatisfaction with the program's results led to experimentation with several reading programs. Not one worked well school-wide. A small group of teachers attended the National Reading Styles Conference in 1994 and "came back so excited" that they started the change process right away. "Their excitement," according to Doris, "became contagious." By the end of the school year, Title I funds were used so that 14 of the teachers could attend

133

a reading styles training session. They wanted more. In the summer of 1995, Park Hills' entire staff began training to become a Reading Styles Model School.

Park Hills' Results

After the first year of reading styles:

- Reading scores increased by 22% across grades 1-4, with an average NCE gain of 3.7 in total reading and 6.3 in reading vocabulary.
- Parents, who were already active supporters, became more involved by making materials and games needed for the children. This involvement increased their awareness of the reading styles philosophy.
- Teachers became more willing to seek and share their own ideas, materials, and information concerning the teaching of reading.
- Park Hills became a Reading Styles Model School, which enabled faculty members to work with NRSI consultants over a three-year period and develop the capacity to serve as a model for other schools nationwide.

Photo courtesy of Park Hills Elementary School, Spartanburg, South Carolina.

An older student concentrates intently on her work. The environment is ideal for her— isolated, quiet, and informal. There's even a healthy snack nearby.

Recomended First Steps

- *Begin slowly and with structure.* At Park Hills, each teacher focused on one component of the reading styles program each month, rather than "just jumping in." Some teachers started recording books, others redesigned their classrooms, some added learning centers and active learning, and so on. Teachers shared ideas and were monitored carefully regarding the component of reading styles they were focusing on for the month.

- *Train the entire staff.* The art and music teachers at Park Hills have also implemented the reading styles program. The music teacher has recorded the words to songs, and the art teacher uses manipulatives to teach new concepts.

- *Extend reading styles to all school activities.* Walk into the school cafeteria at Park Hills at lunchtime and you will see children reading voluntarily. Not only does this activity provide reading practice, but sustained silent reading in the cafeteria is excellent for noise control! The children at Park Hills also present a morning news program each day. The teacher in charge helps them to learn their lines by using the Continuum of Modeling Reading Methods (see Chapter 4). Announcements, news reports, weather reports, birthdays, lunch menus, and poems are read daily. The media specialist and student assistants do choral and echo reading with the children to prepare them for the newscast.

- *Manage student progress.* At Park Hills, reading styles is combined with the Accelerated Reader Program, which helps to structure and manage students' book choices.

- *Share successes.* Updated lists were made at Park Hills to let faculty members know which teachers were working with particular components of the reading styles program. Teachers teamed their efforts and visited one another's classrooms.

- *Provide coaching, feedback, and mentoring.* Some of Park Hills' faculty decided to videotape new strategies. The videotaped lessons were studied and discussed at regularly held faculty meetings. Doris Tidwell and a team visited classrooms often to offer assistance. Successes and problems were shared at building meetings.

- *Continue training.* The reading styles training has been in place for two years at Park Hills, thereby refining and improving classroom practice. At this point, some of Park Hills' teachers are mentoring and helping others.

- *Involve parents.* Park Hills' parent involvement facilitator established a "Parents with Style" group. Members help to make materials such as classroom reading games. The club members make extra games so that they can keep one to take home and work with their own child.

Overall Evaluation

Two years into the reading styles program at Park Hills, the "great majority" of teachers are implementing it at a "high level," according to Doris Tidwell. Some teachers are gradually "coming around." In

Photo courtesy of Park Hills Elementary School, Spartanburg, South Carolina.

Lunchtime becomes sustained silent reading time at Park Hills Elementary. Reading skills improved and the noise level was substantially reduced.

many cases, these are "solid, traditional teachers" who are now finding that they can continue to use methods that have worked well for them in the past, in addition to adopting aspects of the reading styles approach.

Doris feels that one of the greatest benefits of this approach is that it "encompasses many other strategies, while also providing one central focus that everybody in the school can have." And it has "increased the level of achievement" in ways that other approaches by themselves had not.

ROLE OF THE PARENTS

In all three reading styles programs described in this chapter, parents played a key role as supporters of the program and as volunteers who created materials and helped in classrooms. Principals and faculty members trained parents in the reading styles philosophy and techniques. Parents learned about their own global or analytic styles and their own perceptual strengths. They learned how their styles differed from their children, and they learned how to interact more effectively with their own children.

At home, many parents have continued to use reading styles strategies with their children. Having been trained in the use of the RSI, they know their child's reading style, and they understand how to provide him or her with ample reading time, appropriate reading environments, snacks, and mobility. They pair-read and choral-read with their youngsters. They record books for their children if they are able, or they listen to their children read back recorded books brought home from school. Some have learned how to read with those same recorded books!

Most important, in these three reading styles schools, parents are *informed*. They understand why today's debate originated between whole language and phonics, why it persists, and why it wastes energy, time, and money by removing the focus from where it must always be: on the individual child.

Photo courtesy of Park Hills Elementary School, Spartanburg, South Carolina.

Each child listens to a favorite book. This activity improves fluency and reading motivation and helps the youngsters associate reading with comfort, pleasure, and friends.

Profound Results

All three principals in this chapter wanted to improve reading achievement. They began with reading styles training for a core group of teachers. Word spread, and reading styles training was expanded. Every one of the principals was trained in reading styles right along with their teachers, and every one of the principals involved their parents, all the faculty, and other key personnel, such as cooks and custodians.

During the training period, principals evaluated their reading materials, provided the Reading Style Inventory® for all classes, developed banks of recorded books and games to teach specific reading skills, and organized volunteers to work with children and to develop games. Each principal made sure that training, coaching, and feedback were an integral part of the program, and each principal nurtured the teachers throughout the process.

The results were profound. Children's reading achievement improved dramatically. Discipline problems were reduced, and parents became stronger partners. Most important, teachers understood their students better and did a superior job of teaching reading. Pride, ownership, and excitement are evident in all three of these Model Reading Styles Schools.

If You Would Like to Visit. . .

To visit Robb Elementary, R.E. Baker Elementary, or Park Hills Elementary, please write or phone the school to reserve a date. See Appendix B.

REFERENCES

1. M. Carbo, "Every Child a Reader," *American School Board Journal,* February 1997, pp. 33-35; M.M. Kennedy, "Some Surprising Findings on How Teachers Learn to Teach," *Educational Leadership,* vol. 49, 1991, pp. 14-17; and A. Lieberman and L. Miller, *Teachers, Their World and Their Work: Implications for School Improvement* (Alexandria, Va.: Association for Supervision and Curriculum Development, 1984).

2. B. Skipper, "Reading with Style," *American School Board Journal,* February 1997, pp. 36-37.

Georgette (the child for whom the Carbo Recorded-Book® Method was created 20 years ago!) learns to read with a friendly doll named George nearby.

Photo courtesy of Robb Elementary School, Uvalde, Texas.

Faculty at Robb School made this quilt for their school principal,
Diane Crawford. Each square was made by a staff member and depicts
their personality or an incident that occurred during the year.

APPENDIX A

Glossary of Terms

ACTIVE LEARNING - Learning experiences in which the students are active physically, such as touching, acting, and walking (see Chapter 6).

ANALYTIC LEARNERS - Tend to be highly rational, logical, detail-oriented; enjoy highly organized teaching.

ATTENTION DEFICIT HYPERACTIVITY DISORDER (AD/HD) - Students who use motion to bring their central nervous system to a normal state of arousal or alertness (see Chapter 7).

AUDITORY ACTIVITY - An activity that requires of the learner any or all of the following auditory abilities: memory, discrimination, sequential memory.

AUDITORY LEARNERS - Learn by listening and speaking; recall what they hear; usually enjoy discussions.

BILINGUAL (LEP) - Bilingual/Limited English Proficient students are youngsters whose native language is not English and who have not yet achieved mastery of the English language (see Chapter 7).

CARBO RECORDED-BOOK® METHOD - A method of recording small portions of a challenging story at a slow pace to increase students' reading fluency (see Chapter 5).

CHORAL READING - Two or more individuals read a passage in unison. Often verse or patterned language is read by alternating lines or passages (see Chapter 4).

COLORED OVERLAYS - Thin sheets of plastic of special colors that have been found to help many individuals with visual problems.

COOPERATIVE LEARNING - Working in small groups or pairs to complete goals and produce products interdependently.

CRITICAL THINKING - Judging the accuracy, validity, and quality of ideas; using sound criteria, logical analysis, and judgment.

ECHO READING - The teacher reads a line or passage with good expression, then the student(s) read it back (see Chapter 4).

EMOTIONALLY HANDICAPPED LEARNER - A youngster whose behavioral patterns make learning extremely difficult for him/herself and/or classmates (see Chapter 7).

FERNALD READING METHOD - A word that a youngster wants to learn how to read or write is written on a large card by the teacher with a crayon. The youngster traces over and says the word two or three times, and then writes the word from memory (see Chapter 3).

GLOBAL LEARNERS - Tend to be strongly emotional, intuitive, group-oriented; highly responsive to holistic teaching.

INDIVIDUALIZED READING METHOD - This method of teaching reading resembles sustained silent reading in that students spend a good deal of time reading alone. As the children read, the teacher holds individual conferences at which the child reads aloud and discusses what he or she has read. The teacher keeps detailed records of the child's interests and skill levels. Small groups of students with similar reading interests or skill needs may be formed from time to time.

INTEGRATED CURRICULUM - Teaching subject areas, such as science, math, language arts, as related parts of a whole.

INVENTED SPELLING - A writing technique that encourages students to focus on the meaning of what they are writing rather than the mechanics of writing. As children understand and become comfortable with the writing process, they are expected to use correct spellings.

KINESTHETIC ACTIVITY - An activity involving physical movement such as jumping or walking; an activity that promotes learning through large-muscle movement.

KINESTHETIC LEARNERS - Learn through whole-body movement; recall what they experience; often enjoy building, acting, direct experience.

LANGUAGE-EXPERIENCE METHOD - Initially, individuals or groups of students dictate stories about their experiences to their teacher. Later students learn to read what they write themselves about their experiences (see Chapter 3).

LEARNING STYLES - Ways in which people learn. Visual, auditory, tactile, and kinesthetic are commonly known elements (see Chapter 3).

LINGUISTIC METHOD - Word families or patterns (fat, cat, mat) are taught and used in beginning stories (see Chapter 3).

LITERATURE-BASED - A literature-based reading program primarily uses literature to teach reading. Emphasis is placed on high-quality stories, poems, and nonfiction.

MOBILITY - A need some students have to move often as they learn.

MODELING METHODS - A series of reading methods in which a more experienced reader reads and is then imitated by the novice reader (see Chapter 4).

MULTI-AGE - Classrooms in which children of two or more different ages are taught together (sometimes called "nongraded").

NEUROLOGICAL IMPRESS METHOD - The teacher sits behind the youngster and reads into the child's ear as the child attempts to read in unison. The child holds the book and sets the pace by tracing with his/her finger below the words (see Chapter 4).

ORTON-GILLINGHAM METHOD - A multisensory form of phonics that is highly structured and emphasizes tactile input (see Chapter 3).

PAIRED READING - Two people take turns reading the same passage. A variety of pairs can be used, including two students and a teacher and a student (see Chapter 4).

PHONICS - Students learn isolated letter-sounds and then blend them to form words (see Chapters 2 and 3).

READING STYLES - The application of learning style theory to the teaching of reading, with implications for reading instruction (see Chapter 3).

SHARED READING - The teacher reads a story or passage while pointing to the words. Often an enlarged book, a chart, or a passage on a chalkboard or overhead transparency are used (see Chapter 4).

TACTILE ACTIVITY - An activity involving touch, such as tracing sandpaper letters, playing a board game, folding paper; an activity that promotes learning through touching and feeling with the hands.

TACTILE LEARNERS - Learn by touching; recall what they touch; enjoy games and manipulating objects.

VISUAL ACTIVITY - An activity that stimulates the visual sense through color, shape, and other visual stimuli; an activity that promotes learning through sight.

VISUAL LEARNERS - Learn by observing; recall what they see; notice details; enjoy demonstrations.

WHOLE LANGUAGE - A philosophy of teaching reading that emphasizes meaning. Common techniques involve students in reading literature, writing their own stories, using invented spelling (in the early grades), and employing critical thinking strategies (see Chapter 2).

WHOLE-WORD METHOD - Before students read a story, unfamiliar words that will be encountered are introduced often on flash cards, word lists, and in the context of sentences (see Chapter 3).

APPENDIX B

Schools to Visit

This list represents reading programs that exemplify the concepts and major strategies outlined in this book. The list is by no means exhaustive and will be continually updated.

LEVEL 3 MODEL SCHOOLS

Anthon Elementary School
Contact: Mary Helen Diaz
Gonzalez
P.O. Box 1909
Uvalde, TX 78802
210-591-2988

R.E. Baker Elementary School
Contact: Kay Pantier
301 N.W. 3rd Street
Bentonville, AR 72712
501-271-1113

Benson Elementary School
Contact: Mary Helen Saiz
901 Dean Street
Uvalde, TX 78801
210-591-4955

Howard Elementary School
Contact: Pam Zaklan
286 Mace Road
Medford, OR 97501
541-776-8831

O'Connor Elementary School
(Grades 2-5)
Contact: Karen Floro
3204 Bobolink
Victoria, TX 77901
512-788-9572

Park Hills Elementary School
Contact: Doris Tidwell
301 Crescent Avenue
Spartanburg, SC 29306
864-594-4465

Robb Elementary School
Contact: Diane Crawford
715 Old Carrizo Road
Uvalde, TX 78801
210-591-4947

Roosevelt Elementary School
Contact: Ginny Hicks
112 Lindley Street
Medford, OR 97504
541-776-8854

Stemley Road Elementary School
Contact: Vicki Oliver
2760 Stemley Bridge Road
Talladega, AL 35160
205-362-9460

LEVEL 2 MODEL SCHOOLS

Bob Hope Elementary School
Contact: Heidi Mathews
3022 Reforma
San Antonio, TX 78211
210-922-3241

Woodrow Wilson
Elementary School
Contact: Cheryl Meeker
150 East Mendocino
Stockton, CA 95204
209-953-4694

MODEL SCHOOLS IN PROCESS

Dr. Fermin Calderon
Elementary School
Contact: Ricardo Jiminez
P.O. Box 420128
Del Rio, TX 78840
210-774-9968

Gilmer Elementary School
Contact: Pat Camp
P.O. Box 40
Gilmer, TX 75644
903-843-5571

Gilmer Intermediate School
Contact: Paula Hill
P.O. Box 40
Gilmer, TX 75644
903-797-2031

Lamar Elementary School
Contact: Mary Cordova
P.O. Box 420128
Del Rio, TX 78840
210-774-9491

Lincoln Elementary School
Contact: Bruce Wisowaty
410-157 Street
Calumet City, IL 60409
708-862-6620

SCHOOLS TO VISIT

Arizona Fleming Elementary
School
Contact: Brenda Perkins
14850 Bissonet
Houston, TX 77803
713-879-9892

Bachman Elementary School
Contact: Jim Booth
2815 Anderson Pike
Signal Mountain, TN 37377
423-886-0877

Birchwood Elementary School
Contact: Ronnelle Blakenship
Highway 60
Birchwood, TN 37308
423-757-1742

Chatham County Schools
Contact: Beverly Crotts
P.O. Box 128
Pittsboro, NC 27312
919-542-6400

Dupont Elementary School
Contact: Eunice Hodges
4134 Hixson Pike
Chattanooga, TN 37415
423-870-0615

East Brainerd Elementary
School
Contact: Susan Swanson
7453 East Brainerd Road
Chattanooga, TN 37421
423-855-2600

Mary Ford Elementary School
Contact: Brenda Marques or
Therease Metivier
3180 Azalea Drive
Charleston, SC 29464
803-745-7131

Hillcrest Elementary School
Contact: Robert Hope
4302 Bonny Oaks Drive
Chattanooga, TN 37416
423-855-2602

Joseph Keels Elementary
School
Contact: Shirley Henderson
7500 Springcrest Drive
Columbia, SC 29223
803-736-8754

Lincoln Elementary School
Contact: Linda Lee Purcell
458 North Court
Ottumwa, IA 52501
515-684-8031

McBrien Elementary School
Contact: Rodney Thompson
1501 Tombras Avenue
Chattanooga, TN 37412
423-867-6209

Neshobe School
Contact: Peter Mello
RD3 Box 3215
Brandon, VT 05733
802-247-3721

Soddy Elementary School
Contact: Vivian Woods
260 School Street
Soddy, TN 37379
423-332-8841

Spartanburg County School
District #7
P.O. Box 970
Spartanburg, SC 29304
Adult Literacy:
Contact: Marilyn Anderson
864-596-8438
Gifted Education:
Contact: Cindy Henderson
864-594-4400
Model School:
Contact: Doris Tidwell
864-594-4465

CLASSES TO VISIT

Bonnie Bergstrom
Westridge Elementary School
5500 E.P. True Pkwy.
West Des Moines, IA 50265
515-226-2694

Jill Haney
Mark Twain Middle School
2411 San Pedro
San Antonio, TX 78212
210-737-4641

Marsha Carmichael
Edgar Allen Poe Middle School
814 Aransas Avenue
San Antonio, TX 78210
210-227-2591, ext. 3240

Bob King
Westwood Terrace
Elementary School
7615 Bronco
San Antonio, TX 78227
210-678-2780

Rita Foust
Gregory-Portland Intermediate
School
2250 Memorial Parkway
Portland, TX 78374
512-643-4404

Janet Martin
Anson Elementary School
922 Avenue M
Anson, TX 79501
915-823-3361

Janette Norton
Horace Mann Middle School
610 North Buchanan
Amarillo, TX 79107
806-371-5889

Nora K. Robinson
Lubbock I.S.D. Federal
Programs
1628 19th Street
Lubbock, TX 79401
806-766-2206

Caryl Smith
Avondale Elementary School
1500 Avondale
Amarillo, TX 79106
806-354-4490

Lynda Burton-Thompson
Shwab Elementary School
1500 Dickerson Road
Nashville, TN 37207
615-262-6725

APPENDIX C

Publishers and Suppliers of Reading Materials

These publishers and suppliers have materials that NRSI trainers have used and recommend.

RECOMMENDED SOFTWARE PROGRAMS

Prepared by Pat Horn, Curriculum Facilitator,
St. Johns County School District, St. Augustine, Fl.

SOFTWARE FOR WRITING

The Amazing Writing Machine, Grades 2 and Up
by Broderbund (IBM and Mac)

This program provides the fun of a painting program (Kid Pix-like) with a totally customizable word processing program, plus supports for writing when needed. The program offers five options for writing (stories, poems, letters, essays, or journals) and two methods (write or "spins," which are stories in which students can make choices in the wording. For example: I pulled a trick on: my sister, my friend, my teacher, or student-composed text to complete the sentence). The stories print as a book in the story mode or as a letter, etc. The student can customize the page set-up in hundreds of ways, like the text and illustrations in an apple or fish outline. In addition, students are able to access supports for writing at any time. They can get ideas for stories, who, when, where, and why ideas, and many more. It's fun and easy for students to use. The program contains graphics, but they are old-fashioned and limited. This program does not demand a high-end machine as it only requires 4 MB of RAM.

Easy Book, Pre-K to Grade 2
by Sunburst (IBM and Mac)

This program offers a very simple book format for younger writers that is simple to use. The page prints like a book and has a space for illustrating the story.

The Children's Reading and Writing Workshop, Grades 2 and Up
by The Learning Center (IBM and Mac)

This program offers word processing, great clip art, and page set-up features such as text wrap (around pictures).

Bank Street Writer, Grades 2 and Up
by Scholastic

This program offers word processing and many more features. You can also put sound buttons on the document and make linking buttons. For example, if you wish to have text defined, you can make a button that takes you to another window that gives a definition or picture.

SOFTWARE FOR READING

Living Books, Pre-K to Grade 3
by Broderbund (IBM and Mac)

This series of books is wonderful for young readers. The stories are high quality, and the pictures are alive with hidden buttons that have the story characters act out various scenarios. My favorite is the starfish on the beach in "Just Grandma and Me." When you click on him, he does a soft-shoe routine. The buttons may be found by exploring the pictures and further comprehension and understanding.

Reader Rabbit's Interactive Reading Journey, Pre-K to Grade 2
by The Learning Company (IBM and Mac)

This program contains 40 progressively harder storybooks that can be read to the student in many voices, or the student may print out the books to read at home or later for practice.

Storybook Weaver, Grades 1 - 5
by MECC (IBM and Mac)

This program is for reading and writing. There are supports and many graphics relating to themes that interest elementary children. The student sets the scene and then composes the text to match the illustration.

Alien Tales, Upper Elementary
by Broderbund (IBM and Mac)

This program incorporates 30 stories and authors in a game format. The student tries to outsmart a panel of celebrities who claim to have written books. After reading a passage from the book, students must answer questions or solve puzzles.

Eagle Eye Mysteries, Grade 3 - 8
by EA Kids (IBM and Mac)

Great new program that allows kids to read and solve over 50 cases. Fun to read.

MULTIMEDIA

Software to do what we have never been able to do before.

HyperStudio ,**** Pre-K to Adult
by Roger Wagner (IBM and Mac)

If you have no other software, you should have THIS ONE! This program is easy to use, even for the very young. You can use it as a word processing program, a multimedia program with sound, animation, clip art (including an extensive library), buttons and links to go to other programs, video disks, live video, and practically anywhere else. We have kindergartners to high school students who use it for portfolios, reports, welcome to our class stacks, class poetry stacks, and more. You can also access the Internet with this program. It is easy to use, with reminder messages and an intuitive format.

SuperPrint **** Pre-K to Adult
by Scholastic (IBM and Mac)

This program is the best for producing cards, banners, calendars, and posters. It comes with many graphics, most of which are outlines so the students can color them on or off the computer. The print feature automatically allows students to print one page, little books, big books, floor puzzles, or wall posters. Even young children can make cards, banners, and calendars. The program is very intuitive and has multicultural graphics. (This is a must have.)

**** means personal favorites.

BASAL READERS

Whole-Word/Whole Language Emphasis

D.C. Heath – 125 Spring Street • Lexington, MA 02178

Harcourt, Brace, Jovanovich – Orlando, FL 32887

Silver Burdett & Ginn
P.O. Box 2649 • 4350 Equity Drive • Columbus, OH 48228

Phonics Emphasis

Addison-Wesley – 101 5th Avenue • New York, NY 10003

Distar (N-3) – SRA Basic Reading Series – Science Research
Associates – 155 North Wacker Drive • Chicago, IL 60606

Open Court – 315 5th Street • Peru, IL 61354

DRAMA/CHORAL READING

Acorn
Bur Oak Press, Inc. – 8717 Mockingbird Road South • Platteville,
WI 53818

Creative Teaching Press
P.O. Box 6017 • Cypress, CA 90630-0017 • (800) 444-4287

Heinemann
361 Hanover Street • Portsmouth, NH 03801-3912 • (800) 541-2086

Institute for Readers Theater (Plays for K-Adult)
P.O. Box 17193 • San Diego, CA 92117

Oxford University Press (Works by Carolyn Graham)
200 Madison Avenue • New York, NY 10016

ESL

Addison-Wesley Publishing Company
P.O. Box 10888 • Palo Alto, CA 94303 • (800) 447-2226

Scott Foresman
1900 East Lake Avenue • Glenview, IL 60025 • (800) 554-4411

GAMES AND MANIPULATIVES INVOLVING LARGE-MUSCLE MOVEMENT

Frank Schaffer Publications
23740 Hathorne Blvd. • Torrance, CA 90505 • (310) 378-1133
(800) 421-5565

Judy/Instructo – 4424 W. 78th Street • Bloomington, MN 55435

National Reading Styles Institute
P.O. Box 737 • Syosset, NY 11791-0737 • (800) 331-3117
(516) 921-5500

Peguis Publishers
100 318 McDermot Avenue • Winnipeg, MB R3A 0A2 Canada
(204) 987-3500 • (800) 667-9678

HANDS-ON ACTIVITIES, MANIPULATIVES, AND GAMES

Ellison Educational – P.O. Box 8309 • Newport Beach, CA
92658-8209 • (714) 724-0555 • (800) 253-2238

Evan-Moor
9425 York Road • Monterey, CA 93940 • (800) 777-4362

Frog Publications
P.O. Box 280096 • Tampa, FL 33682 • (800) 777-3764

National Reading Styles Institute
P.O. Box 737 • Syosset, NY 11791-0737 • (800) 331-3117
(516) 921-5500

INDIVIDUALIZED PROGRAMS

Book Lures, Inc. – P.O. Box 9450 • O'Fallon, MO 63366-0450

Engine-Unity, Ltd. – P.O. Box 9610 • Phoenix, AZ 86058
(602) 997-7144

Interact – P.O. Box 997 • Lakeside, CA 92040

Scholastic Book, Inc. – 730 Broadway • New York, NY 10003

INTERDISCIPLINARY UNITS

Creative Teaching Press
P.O. Box 6017 • Cypress, CA 90630-0017 • (800) 444-4287

Engine-Unity, Ltd.
P.O. Box 9610 • Phoenix, AZ 86058 • (602) 997-7144

Fearon
P.O. Box 280 • Carthage, IL 62321-0280 • (800) 242-7272

Interact – P.O. Box 997 • Lakeside, CA 92040 • (619) 448-1474

Thinking Caps, Inc. – P.O. Box 26239 • Phoenix, AZ 85068

PHONICS

Carson-Dellosa Publishing Company, Inc.
P.O. Box 35665 • Greensboro, NC 27425 • (800) 321-0943

Modern Curriculum Press
13900 Prospect Road • Cleveland, OH 44136

Steck-Vaughn
P.O. Box 26015 • Austin, TX 78755 • (800) 531-5015

READING KITS

Glass Analysis for Decoding, Easier-to-Learn, Inc.
62 Howard Street • Patchogue, NY 11772

SRA Reading Laboratory – Science Research Associates
155 North Wacker Drive • Chicago, IL 60606

RECORDED READINGS

Acorn
Bur Oak Press, Inc.
8717 Mockingbird Road South • Platteville, WI 53818

National Reading Styles Institute
P.O. Box 737 • Syosset, NY 11791-0737 • (800) 331-3117
(516) 921-5500

SHORT STORIES

Fearon/Janus
500 Harbor Boulevard • Belmont, CA 94002 • (800) 877-4283
Globe Book Co. – 50 West 23rd Street • New York, NY 10010

New Readers Press
Box 131 • 1320 Jamesville Avenue • Syracuse, NY 13210

Scholastic Co. – 730 Broadway • New York, NY 10003

National Reading Styles Institute
P.O. Box 737 • Syosset, NY 11791-0737 • (800) 331-3117
(516) 921-5500

SKILLS DEVELOPMENT BOOKS

(for skills development across content areas)

Carson-Dellosa Publishing Company, Inc.
P.O. Box 35665 • Greensboro, NC 27425 • (800) 321-0943

Center for Applied Research in Education
P.O. Box 105361 • Atlanta, GA 30348

Critical Thinking Press and Software
P.O. Box 448 • Pacific Grove, CA 93950 • (800) 458-4849

Modern Curriculum Press
13900 Prospect Road • Cleveland, OH 44136

SUPPLIES

AccuCut
P.O. Box 1053 • West Highway 30 • Fremont, NE   68025
(800) 228-1670

Callaway House (Inexpensive Room Dividers)
451 Richardson Drive • Lancaster, PA 17603

Ellison Educational
P.O. Box 8309 • Newport Beach, CA 92658-8209 • (800) 253-2238

National Reading Styles Institute
P.O. Box 737 • Syosset, NY 11791-0737 • (800) 331-3117
(516) 921-5500

Jones West Packaging Products (All Sizes Zip-loc Bags)
P.O. Box 1084 • Rohnert Park, CA 94927-9919 • (800) 635-5673

SUPPLEMENTARY READING MATERIALS

Carson-Dellosa Publishing Company, Inc.
P.O. Box 35665 • Greensboro, NC 27425 • (800) 321-0943

Frog Publications
P.O. Box 280096 • Tampa, FL 33682 • (800) 421-2830

Institute for Readers Theater
P.O. Box 17193 • San Diego, CA 98034

Creative Publications
5040 West 11th Street • Oak Lawn, IL 60453 • (800) 624-0822

THINKING

Acorn
Bur Oak Press, Inc.
8717 Mockingbird Road South • Platteville, WI 53818

Creative Publications
5040 West 11th Street • Oak Lawn, IL 60453 • (800) 624-0822

Critical Thinking Press and Software
P.O. Box 448 • Pacific Grove, CA 93950 • (800) 458-4849

Heinemann
361 Hanover Street • Portsmouth, NH 03801-3912 • (800) 541-2086

Thinking Caps, Inc.
P.O. Box 26239 • Phoenix, AZ 85068 • (602) 870-1527

Tin Man Press
Box 219 • Stonewood, WA 98292 • (206) 387-0495

TOPS – 10970 S. Mullno Road • Canby, OR 97013

WHOLE-LANGUAGE RESOURCES

Creative Teaching Press –P.O. Box 6017 • Cypress, CA 90630-0017
(800) 444-4287

Modern Curriculum Press
13900 Prospect Road • Cleveland, OH 44136

Wright Group
10949 Technology Place • P.O. Box 2770 • San Diego, CA 92127

Peguis Publishers – 100 318 McDermot Avenue
Winnipeg, MB R3A 0A2 Canada • (204) 987-3500 • (800) 667-9673

Rigby Education, Inc.
P.O. Box 797 • Crystal Lake, IL 60014

APPENDIX D

Identifying Students' Reading Styles

For More Information:

For a free booklet about RSI research, or to order the RSI, contact NRSI at 1-800-331-3117 or 516-921-5500 • Fax: 516-921-5591 e-mail: nrsi@mindspring.com • P.O. Box 737, Syosset, NY 11791.

Reading Styles Checklist for Identifying Perceptual Strengths

IDENTIFYING AUDITORY STRENGTHS

12-14 = Excellent
 9-11 = Good
  5-8 = Moderate
  0-4 = Poor to Fair

The student can:

___ 1. follow brief verbal instructions

___ 2. repeat simple sentences of eight to 12 words

___ 3. remember a phone number after hearing it a few times

___ 4. recall simple math facts or a few lines of poetry after hearing them several times

___ 5. understand long sentences

___ 6. remember and be able to place in sequence events discussed

___ 7. use appropriate vocabulary and sentence structure

___ 8. pay attention to a story or lecture for 15 to 30 minutes

___ 9. concentrate on an auditory task even when an auditory distraction is presented

___10. identify and recall the sounds of individual letters

___11. discriminate between/among words that sound alike (e.g., "leaf" and "leave" or "cot" and "cat")

___12. discriminate between/among letters that sound alike (e.g., "sh" and "ch" or "a" and "o")

___13. blend letters quickly to form words

___14. sound out words and still retain the storyline

IDENTIFYING VISUAL STRENGTHS

11-13 = Excellent
 8-10 = Good
  5-7 = Moderate
  0-4 = Poor to Fair

The student can:

____ 1. follow simple instructions that are written and/or drawn

____ 2. place four to six pictures in proper story sequence

____ 3. recall a phone number after seeing it a few times

____ 4. concentrate on a visual activity for fifteen to 30 minutes

____ 5. concentrate on a visual task when a visual distraction is presented

____ 6. work on a visual task without looking away or rubbing his/her eyes

____ 7. recall words after seeing them a few times

____ 8. remember and understand words accompanied by a pictorial representation

____ 9. read words without confusing the order of the letters (e.g., reading "spot" for "stop")

____10. discriminate between/among letters that look alike (e.g., "m" and "n" or "c," "e," and "o")

____11. discriminate between/among words that look alike (e.g., "fill" and "full" or "that" and "what")

____12. discriminate between/among letters and/or words that are mirror images (e.g., "b" and "d" or "saw" and "was")

____13. spell words easily that do not have a direct sound-symbol correspondence and must be recalled visually (e.g., "straight," "glue," "knuckle")

____14. read small print and understand drawings with intersecting lines, such as graphs, maps, or musical notes on a staff

IDENTIFYING TACTILE STRENGTHS

11-13 = Excellent
8-10 = Good
5-7 = Moderate
0-4 = Poor to Fair

The student can:

____ 1. draw and color pictures

____ 2. perform crafts such as sewing, weaving, and/or making models

____ 3. remember a phone number after dialing it a few times

____ 4. concentrate on a tactual task for fifteen to 30 minutes

____ 5. hold a pen or pencil correctly

____ 6. write legible letters of the alphabet appropriate in size for his/her age

____ 7. write with correct spacing

____ 8. recall words more easily after tracing over clay or sandpaper letters that form the words

____ 9. remember words more easily after writing them a few times

____10. recall words more easily after playing a game containing those words, such as bingo or dominoes

____11. recall the names of objects more easily after touching them a few times

____12. write words correctly more often after tracing over them with his/her finger

____13. recall words more easily after typing them a few times

IDENTIFYING KINESTHETIC STRENGTHS

10-12 = Excellent
 7-9 = Good
 4-6 = Moderate
 0-3 = Poor to Fair

The student can:

____ 1. run, walk, catch a ball, and so on, in a rhythmical, smooth fashion

____ 2. concentrate for fifteen to 30 minutes during kinesthetic activities that require whole-body movement

____ 3. recall dances, games, sports, and/or directions after performing them a few times

____ 4. move his/her body easily and freely when acting in a play

____ 5. remember words seen on posters and signs when on a trip

____ 6. memorize a script more easily when actually performing in a play

____ 7. understand concepts after "experiencing" them in some way (e.g., going on a trip, acting in a play, caring for pets, performing experiments, and so on)

____ 8. remember words after "experiencing" them (e.g., looking at the word "apple" while eating an apple or pretending to be an elephant while learning the word "elephant")

____ 9. recall words used in a floor game more easily after playing the game a few times

____10. remember facts, poetry, lines in a play more easily when he/she is walking or running, rather than standing still

____11. recall a letter of the alphabet more easily after forming it with his/her entire body

____12. remember the "feeling" of a story better than the details

20 Learning Activities Matched to Students' Perceptual Strengths

Activity	Primary Perceptual Modality(ies)
1. Write a letter to a friend recommending that he/she study this topic. Explain why.	Visual and Tactile
2. Pantomime information you found very interesting.	Kinesthetic
3. Make an attractive book jacket describing information you have learned.	Visual and Tactile
4. Dramatize some of the information after you have explained it. Do this with a group.	Auditory
5. Construct a diorama that illustrates the information.	Visual and Tactile
6. List the facts you learned that you found most valuable. Tell why.	Visual and Tactile
7. Identify two beautiful descriptive passages. Read them to two or three members of your class for appreciation.	Auditory
8. Design costumes for characters you have learned about.	Visual, Tactile, and Kinesthetic
9. Pretend you are a critic. Broadcast a "book review" of the topic.	Auditory
10. Make a crossword puzzle on the information you learned.	Visual and Tactile
11. Have another pupil quiz you on the topic.	Auditory
12. Make a tape recording describing the information.	Auditory

Activity	Primary Perceptual Modality(ies)
13. Make up a game that teaches the topic information.	Tactual and Kinesthetic
14. Dress as one of the people or characters. Tell important facts about yourself.	Kinesthetic and Auditory
15. Write questions you think your class-mates should be able to answer on the topic. Organize a panel participation program.	Tactile and Kinesthetic
16. For historical information, make a time line, listing the dates and events in sequence.	Visual and Tactile
17. Rewrite the information for younger children. Simplify the vocabulary.	Visual and Tactile
18. Construct a diorama with pipe cleaner figures. Describe part of the information you learned about the topic.	Visual and Tactile
19. Construct puppets, and present a puppet show of the interesting information you learned.	Tactile and Auditory
20. For science information, plan a demon-stration experiment.	Tactile and Kinesthetic

Global/Analytic Reading Styles Checklist

SCORING:
Strongly Analytic: 14-18
Moderately Analytic: 9-13
Fairly Analytic: 4-8
Slightly Analytic: 0-3

ANALYTIC STUDENTS OFTEN:

☐ 1. process information sequentially and logically

☐ 2. solve problems methodically and systematically

☐ 3. concentrate and learn when information is presented in small, logical steps

☐ 4. enjoy doing puzzles (e.g., crossword, jigsaw)

☐ 5. like to follow step-by-step directions

☐ 6. can understand a rule without examples

☐ 7. enjoy learning facts such as dates and names

☐ 8. enjoy learning rules and using them

☐ 9. enjoy learning phonics

☐ 10. understand and apply phonic rules

☐ 11. recall letter names and sounds easily

☐ 12. can decode words out of context

☐ 13. can recall low-interest words (e.g., "what," "fan") almost as easily as high-interest words (e.g., "elephant," "monster")

☐ 14. are critical and analytic when reading

☐ 15. can identify the details in a story

☐ 16. recall many facts after listening to and/or reading

☐ 17. list story events easily in logical, sequential order

☐ 18. like to do reading skill exercises

SCORING:
Strongly Global: 14-18
Moderately Global: 9-13
Fairly Global: 4-8
Slightly Global: 0-3

GLOBAL STUDENTS OFTEN:

☐ 1. concentrate and learn more easily when information is presented as a gestalt or whole

☐ 2. prefer to respond to emotional content (e.g., tragedy, humor, fantasy, adventure, etc.)

☐ 3. are attracted to patterns rather than details

☐ 4. get "wrapped up" in a story and do not concentrate on the details

☐ 5. process information subjectively and randomly

☐ 6. need to know the essence of a story before reading/hearing it

☐ 7. need examples of a rule to understand the rule itself

☐ 8. understand "concrete" examples better than those that are "abstract"

☐ 9. can easily identify the main ideas in a story

☐ 10. are less concerned about dates, names, or specific details, unless there is a real need to be

☐ 11. recall information easily when it is presented in the form of an anecdote

☐ 12. will concentrate and pay attention better if the goal of the lesson is clearly stated at the beginning

☐ 13. need to learn with high-interest, meaningful materials

☐ 14. do not enjoy doing isolated skill exercises

☐ 15. are able to learn a reading skill if the lesson is drawn from a story already read

☐ 16. understand better if a story is enhanced by visuals (drawings, cartoons, photographs)

☐ 17. recall high-interest words ("elephant," "circus," "dinosaur") much more easily than low-interest words (e.g., "met," "bet")

☐ 18. use story context to figure out unknown words

Reading Style Observation Guide
from the *Reading Style Inventory* Manual
by Marie Carbo

The following chart takes individual learning styles and needs into account. Teachers can adapt reading strategies so they support students' needs.

Observation	Reading Style Diagnosis	Suggested Strategies for Teaching Reading
The student:	**The student:**	
1. Is distracted by noise, looks up from reading at the slightest sound, places hands over ears, tries to quiet others.	Prefers to read in a quiet environment.	⇨ Provide quiet reading areas such as study carrels and carpeted sections; use rugs, stuffed furniture, drapes to absorb sound; make available headsets to block noise.
2. Can read easily when people talk or music plays.	Prefers to read in an environment with talking and/or music.	⇨ Permit listening to music through headsets while reading; establish reading areas where whispering is allowed.
3. Squirms, fidgets, squints when reading near a window on a sunny day.	Prefers to read in soft or dim light.	⇨ Use plants, curtains, hanging beads, dividers to block and diffuse light; add shaded lamps to reading sections.
4. Seeks brightly lit areas for reading.	Prefers to read in bright light.	⇨ Allow student to read under bright lights and near windows.
5. Wears many sweaters indoors.	Prefers to be in a warm environment.	⇨ Encourage youngster to read in a warmer section of the room and suggest sweaters.
6. Perspires easily; wears light clothing.	Prefers a cool environment.	⇨ Encourage pupil to read in a cooler section of the room and suggest light clothing.
7. Is restless and moves his/her seat when reading.	Prefers an informal design.	⇨ Allow the student to read while sitting on a pillow, carpeting, soft chair, or the floor.
8. Continually asks for teacher approval of reading work; enjoys sharing reading interests with teacher.	Is teacher-motivated.	⇨ Encourage child to discuss reading interests with you and to do reading work and then share it with you; praise him/her; try teacher-directed reading group.
9. Enjoys reading with the teacher.	Prefers reading with adults.	⇨ Schedule youngster to read with you often; try using older tutors.
10. Cannot complete lengthy assignments.	May not be persistent or responsible.	⇨ Give short reading assignments and check them frequently; try multisensory instructional resources.

Observation	Reading Style Diagnosis	Suggested Strategies for Teaching Reading
The student:	The student:	
11. Becomes confused by many choices of reading materials.	Requires structure.	⇨ Limit choices; give clear, simple directions; try a structured reading approach.
12. Enjoys choices, demonstrates creativity when reading.	Does not require structure.	⇨ Provide many choices of reading materials; give many options for project work.
13. Participates actively in group discussions; chooses to read with friends.	Prefers to read with peers.	⇨ Establish areas where small groups can read together; provide reading games, activities.
14. Shies away from others; reads best alone.	Prefers to read alone.	⇨ Provide independent activities such as individualized materials, tape-recorded books, computers.
15. Notices and remembers details in pictures; is a good speller; does not confuse visually similar words ("stop" and "spot") and has a good sight vocabulary.	Is a visual learner.	⇨ Try a whole-word reading approach; if the child also needs structure, try sequential self-checking material.
16. Remembers directions and stories after hearing them; decodes words with ease; enjoys listening activities.	Is an auditory learner.	⇨ Try a phonic or linguistic reading approach; use listening activities.
17. Enjoys learning by touching; remembers words after tracing over and "feeling" them; likes to type, play reading games; is very active.	Is a tactile/kinesthetic learner.	⇨ Try a language-experience approach; use clay, sandpaper, and so on to form words; try many reading games, model building, project work, multisensory resources.
18. Cannot sit still for long reading periods; becomes restless; may misbehave.	May require mobility or different methods.	⇨ Allow student to get a drink or snack and then return to reading work; provide many manipulatives and reading games; try reading on soft couch and/or carpeting.

Elements of Reading Style Identified
By the Reading Style Inventory®

I. Environmental Stimuli   **Does the student read best:**
    SOUND   with music, with talking, or in silence?
    LIGHT   in bright or dim light?
    TEMPERATURE   in a warm or cool temperature?
    DESIGN   in a formal design (hard chair at a desk) or an informal design (soft chair, rug, floor)?

II. Emotional Stimuli   *When reading, is the student:*
    MOTIVATION   self-motivated, not self-motivated, motivated by peers, motivated by adults?
    Does the student:
    PERSISTENCE   complete reading tasks?
    RESPONSIBILITY   do the work agreed upon or assigned?
    STRUCTURE   prefer little or much direction, many or few choices of reading materials, require time limits?

III. Sociological Stimuli   *Does the student read best with:*
    PEERS   five or six students?
    SELF   alone?
    PAIR   one other student?
    TEAM   three students?
    ADULT   a teacher, parent, administrator, etc.?
    VARIED   combinations of students and adults?

IV. Physical Stimuli   *Does the student read best:*
    PERCEPTUAL   when taught through his/her visual modality, auditory modality, tactile modality, kinesthetic modality, and/or with a multisensory approach?
    INTAKE   when permitted to eat and drink while learning?
    TIME   in the early morning, late morning, early afternoon, late afternoon, evening?
    MOBILITY   when permitted to move while learning?

V. Psychological Stimuli   *Does the student:*
    GLOBAL/ANALYTIC   learn best when information is presented holistically (globally) and/or logically, step-by-step (analytically)?

RSI Individual Profiles

RSI Individual Profiles describe a student's reading style strengths and weaknesses, and recommend the most effective reading strategies for that student.

RSI Individual Disks produce RSI Individual Profiles and print descriptions of 14 different reading methods. This disk is consumable and must be reordered after 50 students are entered.

The following two kinds of RSI Individual Profiles can be generated with an RSI Individual Disk:

- **One-Page Condensed Report**
- **Three-Page Complete Report**

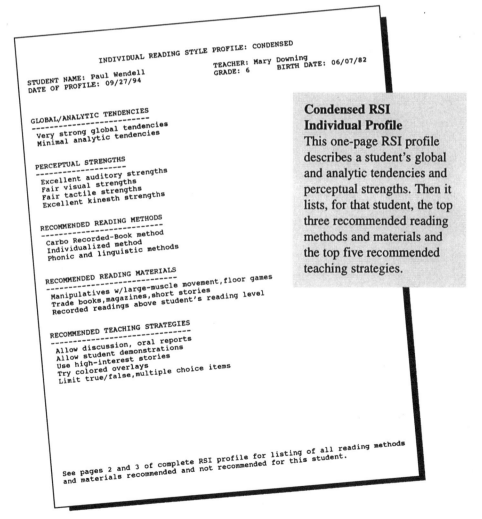

```
                    INDIVIDUAL READING STYLE PROFILE: CONDENSED
                                    TEACHER: Mary Downing
                                    GRADE: 6      BIRTH DATE: 06/07/82
STUDENT NAME: Paul Wendell
DATE OF PROFILE: 09/27/94


GLOBAL/ANALYTIC TENDENCIES
--------------------------
Very strong global tendencies
Minimal analytic tendencies


PERCEPTUAL STRENGTHS
--------------------
Excellent auditory strengths
Fair visual strengths
Fair tactile strengths
Excellent kinesth strengths


RECOMMENDED READING METHODS
---------------------------
Carbo Recorded-Book method
Individualized method
Phonic and linguistic methods


RECOMMENDED READING MATERIALS
-----------------------------
Manipulatives w/large-muscle movement,floor games
Trade books,magazines,short stories
Recorded readings above student's reading level


RECOMMENDED TEACHING STRATEGIES
-------------------------------
Allow discussion, oral reports
Allow student demonstrations
Use high-interest stories
Try colored overlays
Limit true/false,multiple choice items




See pages 2 and 3 of complete RSI profile for listing of all reading methods
and materials recommended and not recommended for this student.
```

Condensed RSI Individual Profile
This one-page RSI profile describes a student's global and analytic tendencies and perceptual strengths. Then it lists, for that student, the top three recommended reading methods and materials and the top five recommended teaching strategies.

Complete RSI Individual Profile (page 1)

```
                        INDIVIDUAL READING STYLE PROFILE
STUDENT NAME: Paul Wendell
DATE OF PROFILE: 09/27/94
                                          TEACHER: Mary Downing
                                          GRADE: 6        BIRTH DATE: 06/07/82
     DIAGNOSIS
     ---------                 RECOMMENDED STRATEGIES FOR TEACHG READG
                               ------------------------------------------   RSI
  GLOBAL/ANALYTIC TENDENCIES                                               MANUAL
  Very strong global tenden.                                              ------
  Minimal analytic tendencies   Teach holistically w/humor,stories,games  P.19#1A
                                Limit routines,rules,directions,details    P.19#2C

  PERCEPTUAL STRENGTHS
  Excellent auditory strengths  Use listening activities
  Fair visual strengths         Limit visual aids: use colored overlays    P.20#3A
  Fair tactile strengths        Limit tactile actvties (writing, typing)   P.20#4C
  Excellent kinesth strengths   Combine readg w/buildg/doing/floor games   P.21#5C
                                                                           P.21#6A

  PREFERRED READING ENVIRONMENT
  Quiet (no music)              Provide quiet areas, carrels, headsets
  Quiet (no talking)            Provide quiet areas, carrels, headsets
  Dimly lit                     Provide shaded lamps, diffused light       P.22#7A
  Cool or warm temp             Temperature isn't a factor for student     P.22#7A
  Formal & informal design      Have hard chairs & soft chairs available   P.22#8B
  Fairly organized              Provide variety of reading materials       P.22#9C
                                                                           P.23#10C
                                                                           P.23#11C
  EMOTIONAL PROFILE
  THIS STUDENT IS:
  Peer-motivated                Encourage share readg interests w/peers
  Not adult-motivated           Don't have share readg intrsts w/teacher   P.23#12
  Not self-motivated            Provide material based on own interests
  Moderately persistent         Provide short & longer-term assignments    P.23#15
  Moderately responsible        Provide some independent work              P.24#16B
  THIS STUDENT PREFERS:                                                    P.24#17B
  Many choices                  Provide large variety of materials
  Some direction                Provide direction as needed                P.25#18A
  Work checked immediately      Check work immediately after completed     P.25#19B
  Work checked by self          Provide some self-checking materials       P.26#20A
                                                                           P.26#21A
  SOCIOLOGICAL PREFERENCES
  To read to a teacher          Schedule student to read to a teacher
  Not to read w/peers           Don't schedule readg activities w/groups   P.26#22
  To read alone                 Schedule sustained silent reading
  Not to read w/peers/teacher   Don't schedule readg groups w/teacher often P.27#24
  To read w/one peer            Schedule paired reading
                                                                           P.27#26
  PHYSICAL PREFERENCES
  Intake while readg            Permit to eat/drink while reading
  Not to read in the morning    Don't schdule reading in morning often     P.27#27A
  Not to read early noon        Don't schedule reading in early noon often
  Not to read late noon         Don't schedule reading in late noon often
  To read in evening            Assign reading to be done in evening       P.27#31
  Much mobility                 Permit to take breaks while reading        P.28#32A
```

Complete RSI Individual Profile, page 1
The first page of this three-page RSI profile lists in detail the student's
reading style strengths and preferences (left column), recommends strategies to accommodate each reading style element (middle column), and
lists the page numbers in the *RSI Manual* that provide more strategies
(right column).

Complete RSI Individual Profile (page 2 & 3)

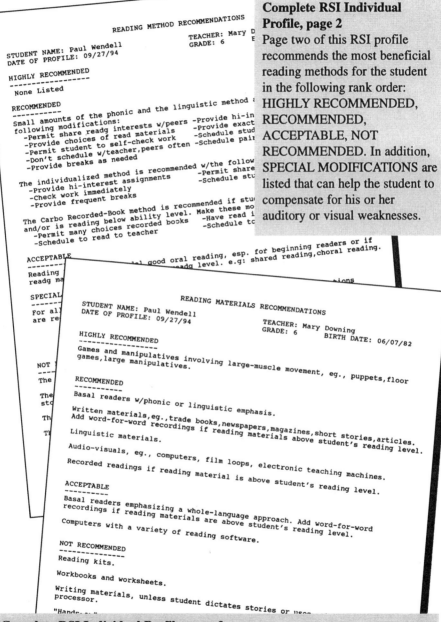

READING METHOD RECOMMENDATIONS

TEACHER: Mary D
GRADE: 6

STUDENT NAME: Paul Wendell
DATE OF PROFILE: 09/27/94

HIGHLY RECOMMENDED

None Listed

RECOMMENDED

Small amounts of the phonic and the linguistic method i
following modifications:
-Permit share readg interests w/peers -Provide hi-in
-Provide choices of read materials   -Provide exact
-Permit student to self-check work   -Schedule stud
-Don't schedule w/teacher,peers often -Schedule pai
-Provide breaks as needed

The individualized method is recommended w/the follow
-Provide hi-interest assignments   -Permit share
-Check work immediately   -Schedule stu
-Provide frequent breaks

The Carbo Recorded-Book method is recommended if stu
and/or is reading below ability level. Make these mo
-Permit many choices recorded books   -Have read i
-Schedule to read to teacher   -Schedule to

ACCEPTABLE

Reading
readg ma   l good oral reading, esp. for beginning readers or if
                            readg level. e.g: shared reading,choral reading.

SPECIAL

For al   ions
are re

NOT

The

The
st

Th

T

Complete RSI Individual Profile, page 2

Page two of this RSI profile recommends the most beneficial reading methods for the student in the following rank order: HIGHLY RECOMMENDED, RECOMMENDED, ACCEPTABLE, NOT RECOMMENDED. In addition, SPECIAL MODIFICATIONS are listed that can help the student to compensate for his or her auditory or visual weaknesses.

READING MATERIALS RECOMMENDATIONS

STUDENT NAME: Paul Wendell
DATE OF PROFILE: 09/27/94

TEACHER: Mary Downing
GRADE: 6   BIRTH DATE: 06/07/82

HIGHLY RECOMMENDED

Games and manipulatives involving large-muscle movement, eg., puppets,floor
games,large manipulatives.

RECOMMENDED

Basal readers w/phonic or linguistic emphasis.

Written materials,eg.,trade books,newspapers,magazines,short stories,articles.
Add word-for-word recordings if reading materials above student's reading level.

Linguistic materials.

Audio-visuals, eg., computers, film loops, electronic teaching machines.

Recorded readings if reading material is above student's reading level.

ACCEPTABLE

Basal readers emphasizing a whole-language approach. Add word-for-word
recordings if reading materials are above student's reading level.

Computers with a variety of reading software.

NOT RECOMMENDED

Reading kits.

Workbooks and worksheets.

Writing materials, unless student dictates stories or use
processor.

"Hands-

Complete RSI Individual Profile, page 3

Page three of this RSI profile recommends the most beneficial reading materials for the student in the following order: HIGHLY RECOMMENDED, RECOMMENDED, ACCEPTABLE, NOT RECOMMENDED.

RSI Group Profiles

RSI Group Profiles describe a group's reading style strengths and weaknesses. RSI Group Disks produce RSI Group Profiles. This disk must be used with an RSI Individual Disk. RSI Group Disks are nonconsumable. The following can be generated: Two-Page Summary Report, 24-Page Names Report, 16-Page X's Report.

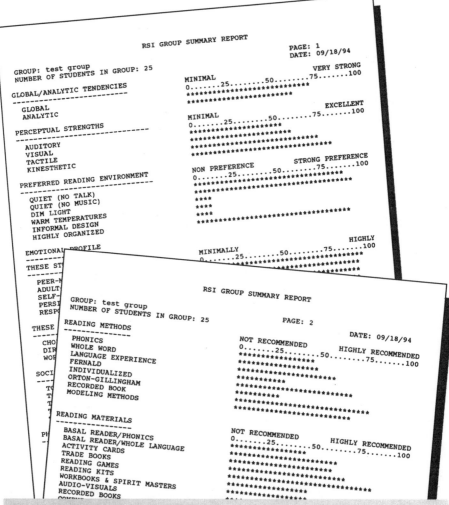

Two-page RSI Group Summary Profile
This profile is produced by the RSI Group Profile Diskette. This summary profile provides graphic representations of the reading styles of the group. This diskette is not consumable and has no student limit. The Group Disk must be used with the Individual Disk.

RSI Group Names and X's Report

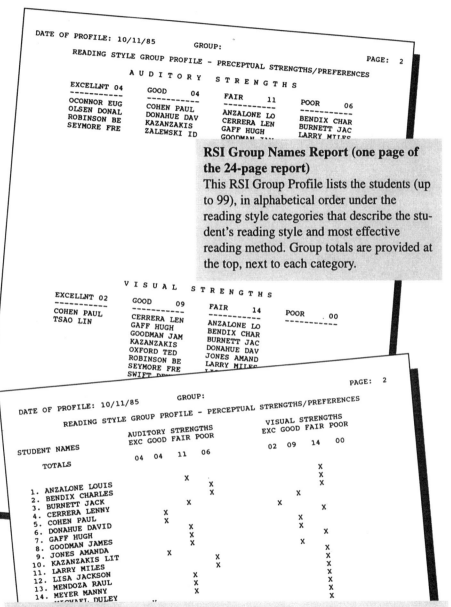

DATE OF PROFILE: 10/11/85   GROUP:

READING STYLE GROUP PROFILE - PRECEPTUAL STRENGTHS/PREFERENCES   PAGE: 2

A U D I T O R Y   S T R E N G T H S

EXCELLNT 04	GOOD 04	FAIR 11	POOR 06
OCONNOR EUG	COHEN PAUL	ANZALONE LO	BENDIX CHAR
OLSEN DONAL	DONAHUE DAV	CERRERA LEN	BURNETT JAC
ROBINSON BE	KAZANZAKIS	GAFF HUGH	LARRY MILES
SEYMORE FRE	ZALEWSKI ID	GOODMAN	

RSI Group Names Report (one page of the 24-page report)
This RSI Group Profile lists the students (up to 99), in alphabetical order under the reading style categories that describe the student's reading style and most effective reading method. Group totals are provided at the top, next to each category.

V I S U A L   S T R E N G T H S

EXCELLNT 02	GOOD 09	FAIR 14	POOR 00
COHEN PAUL	CERRERA LEN	ANZALONE LO	
TSAO LIN	GAFF HUGH	BENDIX CHAR	
	GOODMAN JAM	BURNETT JAC	
	KAZANZAKIS	DONAHUE DAV	
	OXFORD TED	JONES AMAND	
	ROBINSON BE	LARRY MILES	
	SEYMORE FRE		
	SWIFT		

                                                              PAGE: 2

DATE OF PROFILE: 10/11/85   GROUP:

READING STYLE GROUP PROFILE - PERCEPTUAL STRENGTHS/PREFERENCES

| | AUDITORY STRENGTHS | VISUAL STRENGTHS |
| | EXC GOOD FAIR POOR | EXC GOOD FAIR POOR |

STUDENT NAMES	EXC	GOOD	FAIR	POOR	EXC	GOOD	FAIR	POOR
TOTALS	04	04	11	06	02	09	14	00
1. ANZALONE LOUIS			X					X
2. BENDIX CHARLES			X				X	X
3. BURNETT JACK			X					X
4. CERRERA LENNY			X			X		
5. COHEN PAUL		X					X	
6. DONAHUE DAVID		X					X	
7. GAFF HUGH			X			X		X
8. GOODMAN JAMES			X				X	
9. JONES AMAND			X					X
10. KAZANZAKIS LIT		X		X				X
11. LARRY MILES				X				X
12. LISA JACKSON			X					X
13. MENDOZA RAUL			X					X
14. MEYER MANNY			X					X
MICHAEL DULEY								

RSI Group X's Report (one page from the 16-page report)
This RSI Group Profile is produced from the RSI Group Profile Diskette. This profile lists the students (up to 99), in alphabetical order on the left. Their reading style characteristics are indicated by X's under the appropriate heading. Group totals are provided at the top of each reading style category.

175

RELIABILITY OF THE READING STYLE INVENTORY®

A series of test-retest reliability studies were conducted with the RSI from 1981 through 1994, as the instrument has evolved. In the 1994 studies, students were drawn from inner-city, suburban, and rural areas. The samples also represented good, average, and poor readers. A three-week test-retest was observed in each case. These are the results of the most recent studies.[2]

Reading Style Inventory, Grades 1-2

In a sample of 183 first- and second-graders, reliability coefficients for the RSI-P subscales ranged from .73 to .91, with an average of .81. The highest reliability coefficient average was obtained for the perceptual subscales.

Reading Style Inventory, Grades 3-8

In a sample of 216 students in grades 3-8, reliability coefficients for the RSI-I subscales ranged from .69 to .88, with an average of .84. The highest reliability coefficient average was obtained for the perceptual subscales.

Reading Style Inventory, Grade 9-Adult

In a sample of 122 students in grades 9-adult, reliability coefficients for the RSI-P subscales ranged from .61 to .92, with an average of .79. The highest reliability coefficient average was obtained for the perceptual subscales.

RESEARCH WITH THE READING STYLE INVENTORY®

Research in reading styles has demonstrated that the process of assessing and matching students' reading styles results in significant increases on standardized tests of reading achievement. The following section will describe some of the key research findings on reading styles.

Reading Styles Research

Reading Levels After Eight Months of Reading Styles Program for Elementary Students with Learning Disabilities

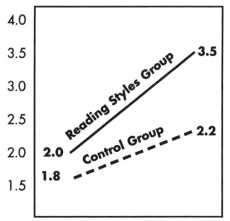

Source: Dr. Lois LaShell, Antioch University, Yellow Springs, OH.

Gains in Reading Comprehension Levels for Chapter 1 Eighth-Graders in Reading Styles Program

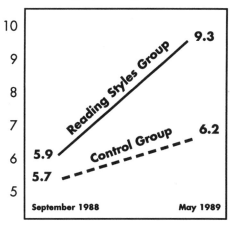

Reported by AnnMarie Romagnoli.
Source: Clarkstown (NY) School District, 1988.

Achievement Scores on the TAAS After Three Years of Reading Styles at Margil Elementary School

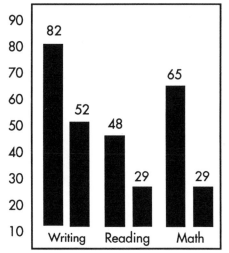

After three years of reading styles, Margil surpassed district scores in all basic subjects on the Texas Assessment of Academic Skills (TAAS). Source: San Antonio I.S.D., TX, 1993.

Average Reading Comprehension Level of 33 High School Special Education Students After Four Months of Reading Styles Program

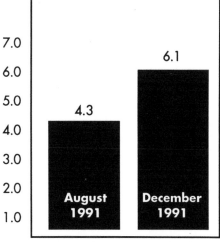

Report of Linda Queiruga's Reading Styles Program at Canyon del Oro High School. Source: Amphitheater School District, AZ, 1991.

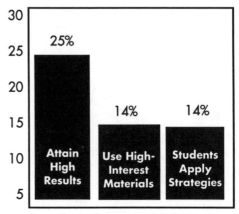

Number of Books Read for Recreation Per School Year for Eighth-Graders

Before Reading Styles	14
After Reading Styles	29

Source: Bledsoe County (TN) Schools, 1991-92.

Percent of Increased Teacher Effectiveness After One Year of Reading Styles Training

Attain High Results	25%
Use High-Interest Materials	14%
Students Apply Strategies	14%

Source: Juanita Elementary School, Lake Washington (WA) Public Schools, 1983.

REFERENCES

1. M. Carbo, *Reading Style Inventory Manual* (Syosset, N.Y.: National Reading Styles Institute, 1993).

2. *The Power of Reading Styles* (Syosset, N.Y.: National Reading Styles Institute, 1995).

3. M. Carbo, *Reading Style Inventory* (Syosset, N.Y.: National Reading Styles Institute, 1982, 1993).

4. A. Snyder, "On the Road to Reading Recovery," *The School Administrator*, vol. 88, 1994, pp. 23-24.

APPENDIX E
Reading Program Evaluation Questionnaire

Use this questionnaire to evaluate and improve your reading program. The questionnaire can be taken before and after implementing recommendations in this book. Pages 183-84 enable you to graph your school's progress.

0 = Never
1 = Seldom
2 = Sometimes
3 = Frequently
4 = Always

DIRECTIONS: *Complete the following questionnaire about your reading program.*

A. BASIC PREMISES

Please circle

1. **Children learn from modeling** (shared reading, recorded books, echo reading, choral reading, reading aloud, etc.).

   0 1 2 3 4

2. **Children enjoy reading and are motivated to read** (lots of voluntary reading, book discussions, book clubs, excitement about books).

   0 1 2 3 4

3. **Learning to read is easy and fun** (variety of reading methods used based on students' strengths, many holistic methods with skills related to stories).

   0 1 2 3 4

4. **Students spend time practicing reading** (time is allocated daily for reading practice, workbooks are de-emphasized, children are read to often, recorded readings are used as needed).

   0 1 2 3 4

5. **The school environment is literacy-rich** (each classroom has a well-stocked library, written language is displayed in many ways [i.e., in hallways and classrooms], stories, charts, poetry, book characters, and authors are discussed and displayed).

   0 1 2 3 4

6. **Parents are actively involved** (workshops are held regularly, information about reading styles is provided, modeling strategies are taught, parents help in classrooms and help create materials).

   0 1 2 3 4

7. **Students are stretched with high-level materials** (challenging materials are read aloud, high-level questions are asked often, thinking is modeled).

   0 1 2 3 4

B. WHOLE LANGUAGE VS. PHONICS

8. The reading program emphasizes global approaches (modeling, literature-based, time for reading alone and with friends).

0 1 2 3 4

9. Children write extensively about what they read and experience.

0 1 2 3 4

10. A variety of decoding strategies are taught (phonics, context clues, structural analysis).

0 1 2 3 4

11. Phonics lessons are brief and tap into global strengths often (singing, tracing, pantomime, games).

0 1 2 3 4

12. Direct instruction in systematic phonics is taught when necessary.

0 1 2 3 4

13. Phonics is de-emphasized with students who are not strongly auditory and/or analytic.

0 1 2 3 4

C. STRENGTHENING READING PROGRAMS WITH READING STYLES

14. Colored overlays are used as needed.

0 1 2 3 4

15. The reading environment is varied and includes areas of soft light and informality.

0 1 2 3 4

16. Students are provided choices that accommodate their preferences (where to sit, with whom to work, how to demonstrate knowledge).

0 1 2 3 4

17. Reading styles are identified with observation techniques, checklists, and/or the RSI®.

0 1 2 3 4

18. Reading styles information is shared with students, other teachers, and parents.

0 1 2 3 4

19. Students' strengths are matched with beneficial reading methods, materials, and strategies.

0 1 2 3 4

D. ACHIEVING HIGH READING GAINS WITH MODELING STRATEGIES

20. Teachers know and apply a variety of modeling reading methods (shared reading, echo reading, choral reading, recorded books).

0 1 2 3 4

21. Modeling methods are used to stretch children as high as possible with challenging reading materials.

0 1 2 3 4

22. Training on the Continuum of Modeling Methods is provided for faculty.

0 1 2 3 4

23. The Continuum of Modeling Methods is used in classrooms.

0 1 2 3 4

24. Teachers provide struggling readers with the amount and kind of modeling needed *before* the children read aloud or alone.

0 1 2 3 4

25. Teachers understand why, how, and when to combine modeling methods.

0 1 2 3 4

26. When students read aloud, they receive sufficient modeling to be fluent and confident.

0 1 2 3 4

E. ACHIEVING HIGH READING GAINS WITH RECORDED BOOKS

27. Teachers have the basic equipment needed to record books (blank tapes, books, recorders, tape players, listening centers, outlets or batteries).

0 1 2 3 4

28. Training on the Carbo Recorded-Book® Method is provided (slow pace, chunking, small amounts, repetition).

0 1 2 3 4

29. Time to record stories and evaluate recordings is provided.

0 1 2 3 4

30. Older students and volunteers are scheduled to listen to children read.

0 1 2 3 4

31. Master copies of tapes are stored. Copies of tapes with the books are sent home regularly to give struggling readers extra practice.

0 1 2 3 4

F. ACHIEVING HIGHER READING GAINS WITH ACTIVE LEARNING

32. The importance of active learning is discussed, and strategies are taught to staff at workshops.

0 1 2 3 4

33. Children are permitted well-managed activity that is separate from learning (stand at desks, move to centers, sit in carpeted areas, sharpen pencils, get a drink).

0 1 2 3 4

34. Children have many simulated experiences as part of their learning (pantomimes, role playing, clap hands for syllables, finding a classmate with the missing half of a compound word).

0 1 2 3 4

35. Games are used extensively to teach or review skills (card games, flip chutes, electroboards, bulletin board games, floor games).

0 1 2 3 4

36. Books with ideas for active learning are available for teacher use.

0 1 2 3 4

37. Volunteers create a variety of games for teachers.

0 1 2 3 4

G. IMPROVING READING TEST SCORES

38. An emphasis is placed on providing a reading program that increases voluntary reading.

0 1 2 3 4

39. Reading styles checklists, observation charts, and the RSI® are used to target instruction throughout the school year.

0 1 2 3 4

40. Alternative assessment strategies are used and evaluated throughout the year (observation, running records, project work).

0 1 2 3 4

41. Reading styles strategies are used during the school year and with practice test materials (students listen to recorded passages from mock tests; they are permitted colored overlays, healthy snacks, and practice of needed skills with hands-on materials)

0 1 2 3 4

42. Teaching objectives are determined based on: lowest scores, need for reteaching, use of methodology that matches students' strengths.

0 1 2 3 4

H. EVALUATING READING PROGRAMS

Please circle

43. Textbooks or reading series are evaluated with a process that includes: quality of material, comprehension instruction, vocabulary, decoding, reading/writing connection.

0 1 2 3 4

44. Students' interests are evaluated and reading materials are provided based on those interests.

0 1 2 3 4

45. Reading fluency is evaluated frequently for flow, phrasing, confidence.

0 1 2 3 4

46. Reading comprehension is evaluated frequently to determine kinds and levels of high-level thinking being taught and modeled.

0 1 2 3 4

OVERALL PROGRAM EVALUATION

A. Basic Premises Incorporated

1. Modeling is provided.

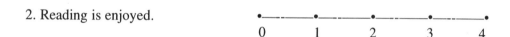

    0   1   2   3   4

2. Reading is enjoyed.

    0   1   2   3   4

3. Reading is easy and fun.

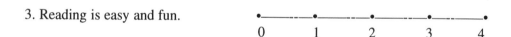

    0   1   2   3   4

4. Reading is practiced.

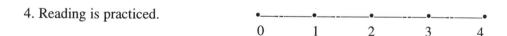

    0   1   2   3   4

5. Environments are literacy-rich.

    0   1   2   3   4

6. Parents participate.

| 0 | 1 | 2 | 3 | 4 |

7. High-level thinking is
   encouraged.

| 0 | 1 | 2 | 3 | 4 |

B. Whole Language/Phonics

| 0 | 6 | 12 | 18 | 24 |

C. Strengthening with Reading Styles

| 0 | 6 | 12 | 18 | 24 |

D. Use of Modeling Methods

| 0 | 7 | 14 | 21 | 28 |

E. Recorded Readings

| 0 | 5 | 10 | 15 | 20 |

F. Active Learning

| 0 | 6 | 12 | 18 | 24 |

G. Improving Test Scores

| 0 | 5 | 10 | 15 | 20 |

H. Program Evaluation

| 0 | 6 | 12 | 18 | 24 |

BIBLIOGRAPHY

Chapter 1

1994 NAEP Reading: A First Look, Findings from the National Assessment of Educational Progress (Washington, D.C.: U.S. Department of Education, Office of Educational Research and Improvement, 1994).

L.W. Anderson and L.O. Pellicer, "Synthesis of Research on Compensatory and Remedial Education," *Educational Leadership,* September 1990, pp. 10-16.

M.R. Binkley et al., *Becoming a Nation of Readers: What Parents Can Do* (Lexington, Mass.: D.C. Heath; Washington, D.C.: U.S. Department of Education, Office of Educational Research and Improvement, 1988).

M.R. Binkley, *Becoming a Nation of Readers: What Principals Can Do* (Boston, Mass.: Houghton Mifflin; Alexandria, Va.: National Association of Elementary School Principals; Washington, D.C.: U.S. Department of Education, Office of Educational Research and Improvement, 1989).

M. Carbo, *How to Record Books for Maximum Reading Gains* (Syosset, N.Y.: National Reading Styles Institute, 1989).

M. Carbo and H. Hodges, "Learning Styles Strategies Can Help Students At Risk," *Teaching Exceptional Children,* vol. 4, 1988, pp. 55-58.

M. Carbo and B. Kapinus, "Strategies for Increasing Achievement in Reading," in R. Cole, ed., *Educating Everybody's Children* (Alexandria, Va.: Association for Supervision and Curriculum Development, 1995).

M.M. Clay, "Introducing a New Storybook to Young Readers," *The Reading Teacher,* vol. 45, 1990, pp. 264-79.

G.S. Fractor, M.C. Woodruff, M.G. Martinez and W.H. Teale, "Let's Not Miss Opportunities to Promote Voluntary Reading: Classroom Libraries in the Elementary School," *The Reading Teacher,* vol. 46, 1993, pp. 476-84.

M.G. France and J.M. Hager, "Recruit, Respect, Respond: A Model for Working with Low-Income Families and Their Preschoolers," *The Reading Teacher,* vol. 46, 1993, pp. 568-72.

J. Johnson, *Assignment Incomplete: The Unfinished Business of Education Reform* (New York: Public Agenda, 1995).

P. Koskinen et al., "In Their Own Words: What Elementary Students Have to Say About Motivation to Read," *The Reading Teacher,* vol. 48, 1994, pp. 176-78.

J.A. Langer and A.N. Applebee, "Instructional Scaffolding: Reading and Writing as Natural Language Activities," *Language Arts,* vol. 60, 1983, pp. 168-75.

L.O. Ollila and M.I. Mayfield, "Home and School Together: Helping Beginning Readers Succeed," in S.J. Samuels and A.E. Farstrup, eds., *What Research Has to Say About Reading Instruction* (Newark, Del.: International Reading Association, 1992).

D.S. Strickland and L.M. Morrow, *Emerging Literacy: Young Children Learn to Read and Write* (Newark, Del.: International Reading Association, 1989).

J. Trelease, *The Read-Aloud Handbook* (New York: Penguin, 1992).

Chapter 2

R. Barr, "Toward a Balanced Perspective on Beginning Reading," *Educational Researcher,* vol. 20, 1991, pp. 30-32.

M. Carbo, "Debunking the Great Phonics Myth," *Phi Delta Kappan,* vol. 70, 1988, pp. 226-40.

M. Carbo, "Deprogramming Reading Failure: Giving Unequal Learners an Equal Chance," *Phi Delta Kappan,* vol. 69, 1987, pp. 197-202.

M. Carbo, "Reading Style: Help a Fairy Tale Come True," *Early Years,* vol. 3, 1983, pp. 10-16.

M. Carbo, "Reading Styles Research: 'What Works' Isn't Always Phonics," *Phi Delta Kappan,* vol. 68, 1987, pp. 431-45.

D. Deegan, "Can We Talk?" *The Reading Teacher,* vol. 48, 1995(a), pp. 704-05.

D. Deegan, "The Necessity of Debate: A Comment on Commentaries," *The Reading Teacher,* vol. 48, 1995(b), pp. 688-95.

E. Kameenui, "Diverse Learners and the Tyranny of Time: Don't Fix Blame; Fix the Leaky Roof," *The Reading Teacher,* vol. 46, 1993, pp. 376-83.

E. Kameenui, "Response to Deegan: Keep the Curtain Inside the Tub," *The Reading Teacher,* vol. 48, 1995, pp. 700-03.

J.M. Newman and S.M. Church, "Myths of Whole Language," *The Reading Teacher,* vol. 44, 1990, pp. 20-26.

"Phonics Ads Cited," *Newsday,* December 15, 1994, p. A64.

R. Rothman, "Balance Between Phonics, 'Whole Language' Urged," *Education Week,* January 1990, p. 7.

R. Rothman, "Studies Cast Doubt on Benefits of Using Only Whole Language to Teach Reading," *Education Week,* January 8, 1992.

P. Shannon, "Response to McKenna, Robinson, and Miller: Whole Language and Research: The Case for Caution," paper presented at the meeting of the National Reading Conference, San Antonio, Texas, 1992.

C. Smith, *Whole Language: The Debate* (Bloomington, Ind.: EDINFO Press, 1994).

D. Spiegel, "Blending Whole Language and Systematic Direct Instruction," *The Reading Teacher,* vol. 46, 1992, pp. 38-44.

D. Spiegel, "Response to Deegan," *The Reading Teacher,* vol. 48, 1995, pp. 696-98.

K.E. Stanovich, "A Call for an End to the Paradigm Wars in Reading Research," *Journal of Reading Behavior,* vol. 22, 1990, pp. 221-31.

R. Turner, "The 'Great' Debate: Can Both Carbo and Chall Be Right?" *Phi Delta Kappan,* vol. 71, 1989, pp. 276-83.

D. Viadero, "Report Casts Critical Eye on Reading Recovery Program," *Education Week,* December 7, 1994, p. 7.

C. Weaver, *Reading Process and Practice: From Socio-Psycholinguistics to Whole Language* (Portsmouth, N.H.: Heinemann Educational Books, 1988).

H. Yopp, "Developing Phonemic Awareness in Young Children," *The Reading Teacher,* vol. 45, 1992, pp. 696-703.

Chapter 3

L. Barber, M. Carbo, and R. Thomasson, "A Comparative Study of the Reading Styles Program to Extant Programs of Teaching Reading" (Syosset, N.Y.: National Reading Styles Institute, 1995).

D. Browne, "Learning Styles and Native Americans," *Canadian Journal of Native Education,* vol. 1, 1990, pp. 23-35.

M. Carbo, "An Analysis of the Relationship Between the Modality Preference of Kindergartners and Selected Reading Treatments as They Affect the Learning of a Basic Sight-Word Vocabulary" (Ed.D. Dissertation, St. John's University, 1980).

M. Carbo, "How to Start Your Own Super Reading Styles Program," *Early Years K/8,* vol. 2, 1984, pp. 46-48.

M. Carbo, "Igniting the Literacy Revolution Through Reading Styles," *Educational Leadership,* vol. 48, 1990, pp. 26-29.

M. Carbo, "Increasing Reading Achievement," *Streamlined Seminar,* vol. 6, 1987.

M. Carbo, "Five Schools Try Reading Styles Programs...And See How Their Kids Have Grown," *Early Years K/8,* vol. 8, 1984, pp. 80-83.

M. Carbo, "Learning Styles: Key to Preventing Reading Failure," *Student Learning Styles and Brain Behavior* (Alexandria, Va.: National Association of Secondary School Principals, 1982).

M. Carbo, "Reading Styles Change from Second to Eighth Grade," *Educational Leadership,* vol. 40, 1983, pp. 56-59.

M. Carbo, "Reading Styles: How Principals Can Make a Difference," *Principal,* vol. 64, 1984, pp. 20-26.

M. Carbo, "Research in Reading and Learning Style: Implications for Exceptional Children," *Exceptional Children,* vol. 49, 1983, pp. 486-94.

M. Carbo, "Research in Learning Style and Reading: Implications for Instruction," *Theory Into Practice,* 1984, pp. 72-76.

M. Carbo, R. Dunn, and K. Dunn, *Teaching Students to Read Through Their Individual Learning Styles* (Boston: Allyn and Bacon, 1991).

E. Chittenden, A. Bussis, M. Amarel, and R. Courtney, "Two Paths Lead to Reading Success," *ETS Developments,* vol. 28, 1982, pp. 1-4.

R. Dunn, "Capitalizing On Students' Perceptual Strengths to Ensure Literacy While Engaging in Conventional Lecture/Discussion," *Reading Psychology,* vol. 4, 1988, pp. 431-53.

R. Dunn, "Commentary: Teaching Students Through Their Perceptual Strengths," *Journal of Reading*, vol. 31, 1988, pp. 15-18.

R. Dunn et al., "A Meta-Analytic Validation of the Dunn and Dunn Model of Learning-Style Preferences," *Journal of Educational Research,* vol. 88, 1995, pp. 353-62.

L. Hart, "Programs, Patterns, and Downshifting in Learning to Read," *The Reading Teacher,* vol. 37, 1983, pp. 5-11.

S.B. Holt and F. O'Tuel, "Reading Styles Program Evaluation," paper presented at the annual conference of the American Educational Research Association, 1990.

J.W. Keefe, "Assessing Student Learning Styles: An Overview," *Student Learning Styles and Brain Behavior* (Reston, Va.: National Association of Secondary School Principals, 1982).

W. James and M. Galbraith, "Perceptual Learning Styles: Implications and Techniques for the Practitioner," *Lifelong Learning,* vol. 4, 1985, pp. 20-23.

L. LaShell, "An Analysis of the Effects of Reading Methods on Reading Achievement and Locus of Control When Individual Reading Style Is Matched for Learning-Disabled Students" (Doctoral dissertation, Fielding University, 1985).

G.E. Mason, "New Software: What'll They Think of Next?" *The Reading Teacher,* vol. 39, 1986, p. 746.

J.E. Oexle and R. Zenhausen, "Differential Hemispheric Activation in Good and Poor Readers," *International Journal of Neuroscience,* vol. 15, 1981, pp. 31-36.

M. O'Hear, "Personality Types and Reading Styles," ERIC # ED 303 778, 1989, 13 pp.

The Power of Reading Styles: Research and Best Practice (Syosset, N.Y.: National Reading Styles Institute, 1996).

L. Queiruga, "A Reading Styles Experiment with Learning-Disabled High School Students" (Syosset, N.Y.: National Reading Styles Institute, 1992).

"Reading Styles: A Model for the Regular Education Initiative," Department of Special Education Forum (Springfield: Illinois State Board of Education, 1990).

R. Restak, *The Brain: The Last Frontier* (New York: Doubleday and Co., 1979).

A. Romagnoli, "A Reading Styles Experiment with Eighth-Grade Chapter 1 Students" (West Nyack, N.Y.: Clarkstown Central School District, 1988).

A. Snyder, "On the Road to Reading Recovery," *School Administrator,* vol. 1, 1994, pp. 23-24.

M. Sudzina, "An Investigation of the Relationship Between the Reading Styles of Second-Graders and Their Achievement in Three Basal Reader Treatments," ERIC # ED 353 569, 1993, 23 pp.

Chapter 4

M. Carbo, "Global/Tactual Learners: How to Teach Them Reading Skills," *Early Years K/8,* vol. 8, 1986, pp. 47-50.

M. Carbo, "Selecting the 'Right' Reading Method," *Teaching K-8,* vol. 27, 1996, pp. 84-87.

M. Carbo, *How to Record Books for Maximum Reading Gains* (Syosset, N.Y.: National Reading Styles Institute, 1989).

G.S. Fractor, M.C. Woodruff, M.G. Martinez, and W.H. Teale, "Let's Not Miss Opportunities to Promote Voluntary Reading: Classroom Libraries in the Elementary School," *The Reading Teacher,* vol. 46, 1993, pp. 476-84.

G. Heald-Taylor, "Predictable Literature Selections and Activities for Language Arts Instruction," *The Reading Teacher,* vol. 41, 1987, pp. 6-12.

R. G. Heckelman, "The Neurological Impress Method of Remedial Reading Instruction," *Academic Therapy,* vol. 4, 1969, pp. 277-82.

D. Holdaway, "Shared Book Experience: Teaching Reading Using Favorite Books," *Theory Into Practice,* vol. 21, 1982, pp. 293-300.

J.A. Langer and A.N. Applebee, "Instructional Scaffolding: Reading and Writing as Natural Language Activities," *Language Arts,* vol. 60, 1983, pp. 168-75.

J.K. McCauley and D.S. McCauley, "Using Choral Reading to Promote Language Learning for ESL Students," *The Reading Teacher,* vol. 45, 1992, pp. 526-33.

D.S. Strickland and L.M. Morrow, *Emerging Literacy: Young Children Learn to Read and Write* (Newark, Del.: International Reading Association, 1989).

J. Trelease, *The Read-Aloud Handbook* (New York: Penguin, 1992).

Chapter 5

M. Carbo, "Advanced Book Recording: Turning It Around for Poor Readers," *Early Years K/8,* vol. 15, 1985, pp. 46-48.

M. Carbo, "Eliminating the Need for Dumbed-Down Textbooks," *Educational Horizons,* vol. 70, 1992, pp. 189-93.

M. Carbo, *How to Record Books for Maximum Reading Gains* (Syosset, N.Y.: National Reading Styles Institute, 1989).

M. Carbo, "Making Books Talk to Children," *The Reading Teacher,* vol. 35, 1981, pp. 186-89.

M. Carbo, "Recorded Books = Remarkable Reading Gains," *Early Years K/8,* vol. 15, 1984, pp. 44-47.

M. Carbo, "Teaching Reading with Talking Books," *The Reading Teacher,* vol. 3, 1978, pp. 267-73.

M. Carbo, "A Word Imprinting Technique for Children with Severe Memory Disorders," *Teaching Exceptional Children,* vol. 11, 1978, pp. 3-5.

C. Chomsky, "After Decoding, What?" *Language Arts,* vol. 53, 1976, pp. 288-96.

C. Thomas and J. Thomas, eds., *Meeting the Needs of the Handicapped* (Phoenix, Ariz.: Oryx Press, 1980).

Chapter 6

A. Bruno and K. Jessie, *Hands-On Activities for Children's Writing* (Old Tappan, N.J.: Prentice-Hall, 1983).

M. Carbo, "How to Play with a Book," *Early Years K/8,* vol. 9, 1979, pp. 68-73.

R. Dunn, *Mobility: A Frequently Misinterpreted Learning Style Characteristic of Underachievers* (Jamaica, N.Y.: St. John's University, Center for Study of Learning and Teaching Styles, 1983).

M. Carbo, "Teaching Reading the Way Children Learn to Read," *Early Years K/8,* vol. 6, 1982, pp. 43-47.

R. Dunn and A. Bruno, "Learning Through the Tactual/Kinesthetic Senses," *Momentum,* vol. 10, 1982, pp. 40-42.

A. Gilbert, *Teaching the Three Rs* (Englewood Cliffs, N.J.: Prentice Hall, 1977).

F. Jaspers, "Target Group Characteristics: Are Perceptional Modality Preferences Relevant for Instructional Materials Design?" *Educational and Training Technology International,* vol. 1, 1994, pp. 11-18.

P. Kaye, *Games for Reading* (New York: Pantheon Books, 1984).

J. Martin, *Sight Words That Stick* (Syosset, N.Y.: National Reading Styles Institute, 1996).

R. Restak, *The Brain: The Last Frontier* (New York: Doubleday, 1979).

R. Thomasson, *Patterns for Hands-On Learning* (Syosset, N.Y.: National Reading Styles Institute, 1993).

M. Valdez, "Improving Reading Skills Through Tactile and Kinesthetic Strategies Within a Whole Language Approach" (M.A. Project, St. Xavier University, 1994).

Chapter 7

R. Barkley, *Attention Deficit Hyperactivity Disorder* (New York: Guilford Press, 1990).

M. Carbo, *How to Record Books for Maximum Reading Gains* (Syosset, N.Y.: National Reading Styles Institute, 1989).

G. L. Flick, *Power Parenting for Children with ADD/ADHD: A Practical Parents' Guide for Managing Difficult Behaviors* (Nyack, N.Y.: Center for Applied Research in Education, 1996).

D. Ford, *Reversing Underachievement Among Gifted Black Students* (New York: Teachers College Press, 1996).

P. Gibbons, *Learning to Learn in a Second Language* (Newtown, Australia: Heinemann, 1991).

A. G. Gilbert, *Teaching the Three Rs Through Movement Experiences* (Englewood Cliffs, N.J.: Prentice-Hall, 1977).

C. Hannaford, *Smart Moves—Why Learning Is Not All in Your Head* (Arlington, Va.: Great Ocean Publishers, 1995).

H. Irlen, *Reading by the Colors: Overcoming Dyslexia and Other Reading Disabilities Through the Irlen Method* (Garden City Park, N.Y.: Avery Publishing Group, Inc., 1991).

P. Kaye, *Games for Learning* (New York: Noonday Press, 1991).

P. Kaye, *Games for Reading* (New York: Pantheon Books, 1984).

P. Kaye, *Games for Writing* (New York: Noonday Press, 1995).

S.D. Krashen, *Bilingual Education: A Focus on Current Research,* Occasional Papers in Bilingual Education, No. 3 (Washington, D.C.: National Clearinghouse for Bilingual Education, 1991).

J. Martin, *Sight Words That Stick* (Syosset, N.Y.: National Reading Styles Institute, 1996).

J. S. Renzulli, *Schools for Talent Development* (Mansfield, Conn.: Creative Learning Press, 1994).

S. F. Rief, *How to Reach and Teach ADD/ADHD Children* (West Nyack, N.Y.: Center for Applied Research in Education, 1993).

R. Thomasson, *Patterns for Hands-On Learning* (Syosset, N.Y.: National Reading Styles Institute, 1993).

K. Spangenberg-Urbschat and R. Pritchard, *Kids Come in All Languages: Reading Instruction for ESL Students* (Newark, Del.: International Reading Association, 1994).

S. Yahnke Walker, *The Survival Guide for Parents of Gifted Kids* (Minneapolis: Free Spirit Publishing Co., 1994).

S. Winebrenner, *Teaching Gifted Kids in the Regular Classroom* (Minneapolis: Free Spirit Publishing Co., 1992).

K. Cummins Wunderlich, *The Teacher's Guide to Behavioral Interventions: Intervention Strategies for Behavior Problems in the Educational Environment* (Columbia, Mo.: Hawthorne Educational Services, Inc., 1988).

Chapter 8

1994 NAEP Reading: A First Look, Findings from the National Assessment of Educational Progress (Washington, D.C.: U.S. Department of Education, Office of Educational Research and Improvement, 1994).

S.R. Angeletti, "Encouraging Students to Think About What They Read," *The Reading Teacher,* vol. 45, 1991, pp. 288-96.

C. Burstall, "Innovative Forms of Assessment: A United Kingdom Perspective," *Educational Measurement: Issues and Practice,* vol. 5, 1986, pp. 17-22.

B. Cambourne and J. Turbill, "Assessment in Whole Language Classrooms: Theory into Practice," *Elementary School Journal,* vol. 90, 1990, pp. 337-49.

M. Carbo, "What Reading Achievement Tests Should Measure to Increase Literacy in the U.S.," *Research Bulletin,* No. 7 (Bloomington, Ind.: Phi Delta Kappa, Center on Evaluation, Development, and Research, 1988).

M. Carbo, "Why Most Reading Tests Aren't Fair," *Early Years,* vol. 3, 1984, pp. 10-16.

J. Johnson and J. Immerwahr, *First Things First: What Americans Expect from the Public Schools* (New York: Public Agenda, 1994).

V.S. Mullis, E.H. Owen, and G.W. Phillips, *Accelerating Academic Achievement: A Summary of the Findings from 20 Years of NAEP* (Princeton, N.J.: Educational Testing Service, 1990).

W. J. Popham, "The Merits of Measurement-Driven Instruction," *Phi Delta Kappan,* vol. 68, 1987, pp. 679-82.

J. Prell and P.A. Prell, "Improving Test Scores — Teaching Test Wiseness: A Review of the Literature," *Research Bulletin,* No. 5 (Bloomington, Ind.: Phi Delta Kappa, Center on Evaluation, Development, and Research, 1986).

R. Thomasson, *Patterns for Hands-On Learning* (Syosset, N.Y.: National Reading Styles Institute, 1993).

D.P. Wolf, "Portfolio Assessment: Sampling Student Work," *Educational Leadership,* vol. 46, 1989, pp. 35-39.

Chapter 9

D. Adams and C. Cerqui, *A Model Textbook Adoption Process* (Seattle: Shoreline School District, 1989).

M. Carbo, "What Every Principal Should Know About Evaluating Reading Programs," *Instructional Leader,* vol. 8, no. 1, 1995, pp. 1-3, 12.

D. Durkin, "What Classroom Observations Reveal About Reading Comprehension Instruction," *Reading Research Quarterly,* vol. 14, 1978-79, pp. 481-533.

Chapter 10

M. Carbo, "Every Child a Reader," *American School Board Journal*, February 1997, pp. 33-35.

M.M. Kennedy, "Some Surprising Findings on How Teachers Learn to Teach," *Educational Leadership,* vol. 49, 1991, pp. 14-17.

A. Lieberman and L. Miller, *Teachers, Their World and Their Work: Implications for School Improvement* (Alexandria, Va.: Association for Supervision and Curriculum Development, 1984).

B. Skipper, "Reading with Style," *American School Board Journal*, February 1997, pp. 36-37.

Appendix D

The Power of Reading Styles (Syosset, N.Y.: National Reading Styles Institute, 1995).

M. Carbo, *Reading Style Inventory* (Syosset, N.Y.: National Reading Styles Institute, 1982, 1993).

M. Carbo, *Reading Style Inventory Manual* (Syosset, N.Y.: National Reading Styles Institute, 1993).

A. Snyder, "On the Road to Reading Recovery," *The School Administrator,* vol. 88, 1994, pp. 23-24.